We need your 2

BARE NAKED BRAVERY

How to Be
Creatively Courageous

♡ *[signature]*

EMILY ANN PETERSON

Book bonuses (recommended resources, videos, articles, worksheets and more) available at www.emilyannpeterson.com/bnb-book

Contents

Why We Need Your Bare Naked Bravery

If you haven't experienced it yet, there will come a day when you need to be brave. Because rainbows die. Unicorns fart. Santa Claus isn't real. Parades get rained on. Shit will hit the fan. It's a fact of life: not everything is as easy as soft serve ice cream with rainbow sprinkles.

I'm not an expert in rainbows, sprinkles or unicorns, but on my eighth Christmas Eve, I delivered a particular piece of bad news about Santa Claus to my younger cousin. So according to my aunt, I'm an expert at raining on parades. I've also gone through more than my fair share of shit hitting the fan.

And so I've had to get brave.

We all know bravery when we see it, but what *exactly* is it? What is it made of? How can we recreate it? When are we truly brave? Who is the bravest among us? Which environments create the most bravery? Is it born or built? Why do we make hero(ine)s from it?

My theory is that Bare Naked Bravery is our fear transcended.

During a particular "season of bravery" in my own life, there were so many days I woke up knowing

I'd have to be brave to keep going, but not knowing exactly how. That's why I wrote this book.

Since you're reading this, I know a couple of things about you. First, you are a rare breed. Not everyone is interested in being brave or courageous. Entire generations are content to build safety nets, lie back and let life happen to them. Entire industries exist for people who escape the reality of their own lives by watching other people's because facing their own is too terrifying. I don't think you're interested in living that way.

Second, despite all the awful, terrifying things happening in the world, there's something calling you to be more than your fear or discomfort. Maybe you have a Pinterest board or desktop file titled "Hop To It, Houdini" and it's filled with elaborate escape (vacation) plans and quit-your-job ideas. Heck, maybe you just lost that job. Maybe it's getting hard to breathe in certain situations, to get out of bed, or to cope with the loss of a friendship, a lover, or a family member.

That sucks. All of it.

Yet you perform daring feats of heroism (like pay rent tomorrow or plan the funeral in three days) or nudge yourself gently toward a new chapter of life (like acknowledging the eventual breakup of your relationship).

When you do so, you're calling on Bare Naked Bravery—using the fear and limitations life hands you to build something better.

Here's what I know: through the layers of our fears, the potential for Bare Naked Bravery exists. Through every layer of life's dream-crushing restraints, courage still exists.

Bare Naked Bravery is not the permission to live without fear. Nope, Bare Naked Bravery gives us permission to move forward—through our fear—with vulnerability, imagination and improvisation in creative ways.

We can strengthen the ability to use fear beyond the impulses of fight or flight. The benefits of being vulnerable and strong lie in freedom of choice: we don't have to run away from something, nor do we have to struggle so hard to attain that which we desire.

The trick is to accept and live within our constraints, whether time, money, confidence, friends and family, education, emotional and physical challenges … the list could get pretty long. A key to Bare Naked Bravery is to embrace the limitations. They define your playing field. They point you in the right direction and keep you from stepping out of bounds.

Building your bravery will remind you that constraints have a good side and fear is on your side. It's true. I gladly yet with great trepidation encounter bravery daily. Using constraints creatively is practically my profession.

I am a creative consultant and teaching artist. When I teach creative workshops or retreats, I see the fear in my students' eyes when they face a new assignment.

They clutch their instruments or notebooks, recoiling as if the extra 6 inches of distance from the assignment actually make a difference. Then I watch fear melt into bravery as the class moves forward one step at a time.

As a singer/songwriter, the personal limitations of the stage are significantly more frightening and more frequent. I have my own battle with stage fright. But the threats and constraints of the stage are all worth it when I get to hear stories about Bravery from my audience members. After concerts at the merchandise table with my lovely fans I hear over and over again in various forms, how grateful they are that I chose to be brave that night so they could hear those stories and sing those songs together. More often than not, they are thanking me for the reminder that they are not alone.

My career aside, I have personally gone to unhealthily great lengths to avoid experiencing the immense pain from my fear of abandonment and even my fear of beauty. I've even feared love. I have crumbled under the weight of perfection and failed miserably. I have scars from an eating disorder. I have clocked years of time being brave with therapists in recovery. And while we're talking about low moments, let's be honest. I have literally and metaphorically knocked over coffee mugs and cried like a baby over spilt milk.

Since writing this book a couple of things about me have changed.

1. I know *how* to be brave because I know exactly what bravery is made of.
2. Constraints are fascinating and not an automatic death sentence for my dreams.
3. Curiosity is a way of life.
4. Feeling fear is not as terrifying as it used to be.

Researching the subject matter of this book prompted me to start a podcast. Kind of an off-the-wall thing for a musician to do seemingly spontaneously but I had reasons for this. In my research, I kept having all these really mind-blowing conversations with people I admired. Boiling their stories down into a simple quote in a book didn't seem fair, to you or to their bravery. Each episode holds stories and conversations that deserve to be shared with the world. (Go binge-listen to as many episodes as you'd like! http://barenakedbravery.com)

Despite the admiration I have for the courageous stories featured in each podcast episode, I chose to *not* to mention my guests' stories of bravery here in the name of vulnerability. Not so coincidentally, vulnerability is the first ingredient of bravery we will unfold in the following chapters. In the name of "being brave" I chose to bare it all in the following pages. Sprinkled throughout these pages you'll find stories of my own I haven't told many folks yet, chosen with the utmost intention to practice what I preach.

How to Use This Book

Part One dives into the relationship between creativity and courage. You'll learn what bravery looks like when we're at the very end of our metaphorical rope and how bravery doesn't always look as valiant as jumping into a burning building. You'll learn about the three types of bravery (internal, external and resonant) and why knowing the difference between them can empower your own bravery. You'll also learn the three most potent reasons why we do brave things and how to bolster our brave intentions to make bravery easier.

In Part Two you'll learn about the 12 ingredients for bravery, starting with: Vulnerability, Imagination, and Improvisation. You'll also learn about the benefits of boundaries, how they assist in our risky choices. You'll find out how context informs how honest you can be in a given situation. You'll learn why we need defiant expectation and a vision of possibility if we are to break through externally enforced standards and realistic limitations. You'll learn how to use the friction of our limitations with the guidance from your intuition. You'll learn how to identify and regain your power choice to flip victimization on its head.

You'll get a primer on how to build your own bravery in Part Three. You'll discover the five characteristics of a powerful daily practice of building bravery and the five gifts found with that daily practice.

14

You'll learn my four favorite bravery building tools for your daily practice. We'll dive into the benefits of fostering your freedom of expression, how to enhance your imagination, and how to strengthen your improvisational skills with these new bravery building tools.

In the back of the book, you'll find recommended resources for further curiosity, a book club guide, a series of questions to boost your bravery almost instantly. Downloadable versions of those resources are available in the book bonuses available here: http://emilyannpeterson.com/bnb-book

Since we don't get to consume musical lyrics as often as we used to, in the back of the book I've nestled lyrics to a handful of original songs inspired by moments of bravery I've witnessed and prompted by people who make me feel brave. Drink them in slowly, preferably 3-5 minutes at a time.

More importantly I encourage you to breathe in the words held in these pages. Allow them to expose your intentional practice of building Bare Naked Bravery. You're invited to join me and the rest of my community in celebrating the reality that our fears can become our allies and our constraints are extremely powerful tools to carve a beautiful life, even when the world is literally melting around our ankles.

Before we go any further, let's get a couple of things straight: Though the subtitle of this book has the word "creative" in it, this is not a how-to-be-a-creative-person book. It's not about how to make more art. And it's not about how to reinvent yourself. The collection of text and words you hold in your hands is about how we can build our bravery instead of wasting our life away wallowing in avoidance of, victimization from, and struggle with our fears and constraints.

When we are fluent in Bare Naked Bravery, life's constraints become catalysts for all the things every self-help book, armchair therapist, and life coach has ever wanted to give you: growth, empowerment, grounded decisions, calmness, clear boundaries, aligned chakras, healthy digestive tracks, wallets filled with low credit scores, blah, blah, blah...

I'm not promising those things, because all that is still on you. (You don't get off the hook that easily. Nice try.) But I will say this: When channeled through the ingredients of Bravery, our fears and constraints make things happen, in big and small ways. When we understand more clearly why we do brave things, it's a bit easier to do them. When we begin a daily practice of building bravery, bit by bit it gets even easier.

Bare Naked Bravery doesn't play favorites, we *all* have it. Bravery has no political leanings or sexual preferences, so you can go ahead and fold up your over eager flags of cultural pride. Bravery doesn't judge our resumes or salaries, so file away your pay stubs until April or jam them in a trusty shoebox. It doesn't do background checks, because it knows history doesn't have to repeat itself. Bravery doesn't keep track of our credit scores, thank God. It isn't always fancy or glamorous, because it likes a good pair of sweatpants just like the rest of us.

Each of us is born with the capacity for Bravery. Congratulations! You made it this far. You're not dead yet! The school of life has already taught you some basics of bravery whether you realize it or not. Bravery doesn't play the lottery, it is a skill built upon experience, resilience, expression, mindfulness, and resourcefulness - it is the practice and mastery of using constraints in innovative ways.

Even though we all have the capability for it, the practice of Bare Naked Bravery is necessary, because building the skill requires the intentional nurturing and expertise that only the ingredients mentioned in the remaining chapters can give us.

As much as I wrote this book for you - and believe me, I did - every word and every sentence was also written to remind myself how to build upon my own Bravery. So hear this when I say, I am with you in your fears and constraints. I know they suck. I know they're scary beyond belief. I know they knock the wind out of life. But I also know they don't have to.

Every day you spend wallowing in the victimization of how terrible your life has turned is a day you've wasted on stagnant strife, pining over what could've been, and denying all that still can be. I'm speaking from experience and it's not fun.

Don't waste your constraints. Keep reading. It's worth it. You are worth it. And as crazy as this might sound, your fear is worth it too.

We need you to show up, speak up, stand up. We need your vulnerability. We need your imagination. We need your improvisation.

We need your Bare Naked Bravery.

Part One

The Cycle of Creativity & Courage

As told through an eviction & diagnosis

> *"Perfection is achieved not when there is nothing more to add, but when there is nothing left to take away."*—*Antoine de Saint-Exupery*

My right hand reminds me every day I am less than 36 inches away from my fear at all times.

The cello became my second voice starting in elementary school by way of practicing for countless school and city youth orchestras, not to mention private lessons every week. I spent a lot of time honing my ability to communicate via bow. My cello got me scholarships to colleges across the U.S. I lugged my cello across the country, through venues, performance halls, and teaching studios. To this day, there is a small part of my subconscious reserved for knowing where my cello is at all times. Like I said, second voice.

My early 20s were spent playing in orchestras while pinging around music industry jobs in Seattle. Music licensing wasn't engaging. Record labels were just widget salesmen with their own personal warehouse. Intellectual property law was fascinating, but I hated filing paperwork. Venues were raking the musicians over the coals of their miserable profit margins.

Realizing I didn't want to sell, scrounge, or exploit music, I fessed up: I wanted to *make* the music.

So I turned my skills as a cellist into a full-time, self-employed career. I worked hard and loved every second. I spent at least 80 hours a week running my business, teaching students, booking recording sessions and playing weekend gigs. I was grateful to have found a job so holistically rewarding. It was a dream come true and my cello was always by my side.

I didn't want to change a thing. Well ... I wanted to change just one thing.

Music students had a tendency to drop like flies during the summer and the holiday season. I thought yearlong contracts were a brilliant idea. (I still do) because, why on earth would I waste time seeking new students when I've already committed my schedule to the students who committed to me in a legally binding way? My students agreed and they signed 12-month contracts for membership to my teaching studio.

Generally, I highly suggest this business structure to private teachers out there. But only after telling them what happened next.

One lady signed the largest contract option available. She wanted cello lessons twice a week for a year. After a two months of paying me a LOT of money, she vanished. Wouldn't return my emails. Wouldn't return my phone calls. Though she was contractually obligated to pay me (or arrange for something else,) she ghosted with absolutely no warning and no explanation.

Ta daaa! My monthly personal income was now short two thirds of rent. I knew shit was going to hit the fan if something didn't change.

The nerve of this lady. Because of her inability to follow through, or even communicate why she couldn't follow through, I officially couldn't afford my rent. After a couple of months desperately trying to replace the income, I had 20 days to let my landlord know.

Fortunately my landlord was also a friend. She told me, "Emily Ann, courage rarely feels courageous. You've got this." She was right. I packed up my stuff and moved into a friend's guest bedroom.

Little did I know, this self-eviction would be the first of many dominos to fall that season.

Earlier that year, I began to notice a small trembling in my right hand, the hand that holds my cello bow. Thinking it was just from too much coffee or maybe my imagination, I ignored it. I kept ignoring it until I began to notice *other* people trying to ignore it.

We'd be having a perfectly engaging and normal lunch conversation, and I'd watch my friends' eyes steal a glance at my trembling hand. It was most severe when I tried to hold chopsticks, a fork, a spoon or talk with my hands, which I do a lot. The trembling made me look like I was nervous, even though I wasn't.

"I'm not doing it on purpose. My hand just shakes sometimes," I would say as if I tried to hide a full-grown pink elephant with a baby's blanket. The shaking wasn't in my imagination.

It went harmlessly like this for months. Until ...

While warming up in preparation to teach a cello lesson, I heard it. The tremble. The hand tremor became audible. Ever so slightly my cello shook, sounding like a terrified whisper from inside the strings. I called my general practitioner immediately. She saw me the next week and practically held my hand as we walked upstairs to the neurologist's office. She was concerned, more than I was.

It was nothing. Surely it was nothing. It was simply too much stress. The recent self-eviction and living in a guest bedroom were just making me feel uneasy about life. Despite my attempts at explaining it away, there was a small voice in me suggesting, "Perhaps this is why you're so exhausted at the end of a teaching day lately? Maybe you've been subconsciously trying to wrestle your bow to stay steady for more than eight hours every day?"

The neurologist confirmed that yes, I have a degenerative, hereditary, neurological disease called an Essential Tremor. I left with a prescription and the whole of the internet at my trembling fingertips.

A couple of weeks later, at my third neurological appointment, the doctor was consoling me after our second failed medication attempt. Minimizing my hand tremor was proving harder than he had thought and I thought he was making a bigger deal than necessary until he said,

"Emily Ann, we need you to keep playing music. I need you to keep playing your music. *You* are the kind of neurology patient who gives me a reason to come to work. The world needs more music. We will find something for you. Let's try this other medication ..."

I don't remember what he said next because that was the moment it hit me.

I had already done my online research. Essential Tremors are degenerative. The shaking in my right hand was going to get worse, not better. I knew there was (and still is) nothing but symptom fixers out there as a treatment. There is no cure. The shaking might even spread to other body parts.

The reality of my impending loss finally broke through denial, like a tons of bricks tied to my cello falling from a cliff. They hit the ground hard. Shards of hand-carved, hand-varnished spruce and pine lay on the godawful hospital carpet under my feet. Here I was helplessly sitting on some butcher paper in a windowless hospital room. I could do nothing about it. I felt as splintered as my career would inevitably become.

Looking up from my feet to his face I interrupted my neurologist. "So … this isn't just going to go away, is it?"

He sighed. Looked up from his prescription pad to meet my eyes, finally saying, "No. I'm so sorry. It's not going away."

I was now staring my humble but beloved cello career in its dying eyes.

So yeah. Rainbows die. Unicorns fart. Santa Claus isn't real. Shit will hit the fan. Fear is a fact of life and I was drowning in constraint.

"Who would I become without my cello next to me? Would that even be enough? What would I do now?"

I had already reluctantly evicted myself because a student bailed on her tuition. I was living out of my car and sleeping at a friend's house. Not only that, but for months, I had scraped together and raised enough money for a six-week Artist Residency which was to start in two weeks.

An arts organization selected me to spend my time in the mountains recording new music—new music for the cello. But how could I do that now? I was too furious. I was burnt out. I was so tired of holding my hand still, all the [BLEEP]ing time.

Yet still it shook. But now it not only shook from my mucked up neurology, but also with fury, grief and fear.

Defining Creativity & Courage

By reading this book you're not being asked to quit your job and start wearing jeans with paint splatters. Nor are you being asked to go rent a studio space or start taking 'artist 101 classes.' And if you are a beret-wearing, pipe-smoking, bitter poetry professor hanging out at a local university coffee shop, fret not! You are not being asked to shed your "Artist" label.

But before we get any further, let's get this out of the way: There is no Creativity Club. Creativity cannot be restricted to a single place or person. It does not require paint nor a musical instrument nor a student loan.

Creativity is having the character of novelty. It is newness. It is a raw moment, a fresh connection. It is a unique mindset or worldview. It is a never-been-done-before solution. When the human race evolves, we are collectively creative. By making an agreement with the world to live a life bigger than the one we had in our mother's womb, we are creative. Every day after that first day of life is merely evidence that we are creative.

This may seem too 'wide' a term to apply to creativity, but creativity can also be a tailored process. By tailoring a process you're not reinventing the wheel from scratch. Only one part, only one angle, only one new sliver is required—just enough to break the standard of normal. Just enough to possess potential. Because to possess creativity is to possess potential and creativity doesn't have to be 100 percent original.

We use creativity daily when we think beyond the status-quo, by entertaining questions that start with, "I wonder..." or "Does it always have to...?" or "How could we change...?" When your thoughts bump up against the standard of normal or even threaten to bust up the norm—that is Creativity at work. Simply entertaining the nudge for a new thought or question is creativity at work.

Here's the cool part: The slightest amount of creativity implies the tiniest amount of courage. Even the act of entertaining the mere notion that you would possess creativity, even *that* requires the tiniest amount of courage. At its core, being courageous threatens a sense of 'normal'—yours or someone else's—with definitive action.

Being courageous creates—even (and especially) when you don't feel very courageous.

The very nature of courage and creativity imply a cycle.

Creativity implies newness. Newness requires doing something differently. To do something differently requires courage. To have courage provides a measure of empowerment to do something unique.

If I sound like I'm talking in a circle it's because I am. Creativity begets courage. Courage begets creativity. Repeat ad nauseam.

They lean on each other. They feed off each other. The spiral starts ever so small. So small that when you're looking at just the beginnings of it, the courage might not look or feel like much. But over time, if you nurture creativity and courage, you'll see them spiral and splay into a wide net of what we later identify as great feats of bravery or even small glimmers of hope.

Before receiving that fateful news in my neurologist's office, I had already decided to take my keyboard to the Artist Residency. Even though the six weeks of hibernation was originally intended for writing pieces for the cello, I planned to have the keyboard there for reference and for more recording options, should I want to add additional color to the pieces I was planning to write. I knew enough about music theory to make some pretty decent chords on the piano. That was before the diagnosis.

What followed the diagnosis in those mountains was six weeks of writing songs for voice and piano. I did not touch my cello. Instead I creatively sulked and shoved my cello up against wall like a piece of unused furniture. Those six weeks were the longest I had gone without touching the cello since elementary school. It just sat in the corner. I couldn't bring myself even to run the bow across the strings, not once. Its rounded steel alloy strings could've ripped my pain like a dull knife. That would've hurt less than it already did.

So I used the time in the mountains to sulk, take some walks, and because I had an agreement with this arts organization, I wrote some songs. My stubborn grief revealed that my remedial piano playing skills were perfect for my tremor. I could bang out chords and karate chop the keys fairly accurately without much excess stress or difficulty, unlike holding a cello bow.

Not all the songs had my stamp of musical approval—we are all our own worst critics—but there were several songs I finished and said, "Huh. That's not too terrible. I'm not half bad at this songwriting thing." The constraints of my tremor, my solitary surroundings, and the new tools at my fingertips garnered enough Bare Naked Bravery to get me through the six weeks of hibernation and grief.

Like a beardless Moses, I descended from the Cascade mountain range with a new plan and handfuls of sad yet sassy and somewhat scandalous pop songs. I ended those six weeks with a long road of grief and many layers of transition ahead, but with enough songs to know that I was more than a cellist. I always had been.

The way everything unfolds through time has shown me repeatedly that even though life can look different from what I would imagine, when my vulnerability overlaps with imagination and improvisation, there lies my Bare Naked Bravery.

No, we cannot blink our eyes and suddenly be done with our struggles. No, we cannot rub a genie lamp and have decades of habitual negative thoughts vanish. No, we cannot hold our breath and expect the fear to go away on its own. Neither can we force our way through life, muscling out our expectations of success or failure. (Besides, muscled success never feels like the success we truly desired anyway.)

There is no unicorn horn that will magically fix your life; if there is, it's called Bare Naked Bravery. We are all born with the potential for it; it is a learned skill built upon vulnerability, imagination, and improvisation. To grow any skill, especially the skill of Bravery, we must first nurture an environment for it.

Let's talk about what this cycle of creativity and courage looks like when you're at the end of your rope and can't see a way out of your situation, because those are the moments when bravery feels its most unattainable. Those are the life or death moments that weigh on and prevent us from seeing how Bare Naked Bravery is still there, diligently at work.

Between a Rock & a Hard Place

"You may encounter many defeats, but you must not be defeated. In fact, it may be necessary to encounter the defeats, so you can know who you are, what you can rise from, how you can still come out of it."—Maya Angelou

Okay, so what is Bare Naked Bravery when you're so exhausted your yearly cortisol secretions have capped out in early February? What happens when your hierarchy of needs has been flipped on its head? What does it look like to have bravery when you're at the end of your goddamned rope and shaking like a leaf?

My years of teaching music proved repeatedly that with the right environment, even failure can foster success. I saw my students come to their lessons thinking they had failed all week in practice time at home, only to sit down and play a song infinitely better than the week before. They had improved and grown, not simply because they failed, but because of the *way* they failed. Steady improvement equals success for any student, especially for students of bravery.

But rarely do we flaunt the mistakes and failures required for success. Rarely do we even acknowledge them. We don't *celebrate* the mistakes like I encouraged my students and now encourage clients.

Take for instance, a business featured in Fortune magazine or a social media influencer traveling the world. It's easy to forget that the profits or web analytics are merely a representation of the daily dedication and the pile of experimentation and failure that it takes to run a successful business.

Each of us is presented with a unique set of limitations, obstacles, and feats of bravery. Listening to so many stories of bravery in all shapes and sizes, I've seen first-hand that just because someone else's pain or tragedy seems bigger than our own does not negate our unique experience of that pain and tragedy.

There's something about that shared retelling of painful experiences and feats of bravery that levels the playing field for everyone listening, regardless of the degree to which each has experienced pain. By sharing the stories that tug on our heartstrings we nurture a communal environment for our individual pain to heal and transform.

There were times in my life when my environment felt anything but nurturing, but even in those constraints Bravery still existed. Dare I say even thrived. Though my heart still breaks for my younger self, when I look back on them I can see Bravery peeking out like the bud of an ivy vine growing between the cracks of a brick wall.

By the time I was in seventh grade, public school was a charade. I knew it. You could not (and still cannot) pull the wool over my eyes. That's always been one of my super powers. Us middle school students were getting shuffled around, herded from class to class like Texas cattle. I was not okay with it. Besides, it was junior high. It was awful all around and I wanted no further part in it. So at the end of that year, I begged to be homeschooled.

Since mom had homeschooled us (myself and two younger sisters) a couple years previously, she took the challenge again and began homeschooling her junior high daughter. I was in eighth grade. It went pretty well, all things and hormones considered.

My parents went through my "report card" verbally. About every six months we'd sit at the kitchen table and talk, just the three of us, about every topic in school. Here's how those conversations would go...

Dad would usually take a deep breath and start in, "Emily, we're so proud of all that you're doing."

Pause.

"Math is great. Science is going really well. Your English papers and literature reading are truckin' along and you're doing so well in orchestra and with private cello lessons, but ... we're worried you're not getting enough P.E."

Laughably, I was concerned that I wasn't "making the cut" as a homeschooler. When the only competition for valedictorian is yourself, you listen when someone says your attempts at being yourself is not enough.

So I tugged on the thread of this report card statement by asking a few more questions of mom and dad. What unraveled was their true, unadulterated opinion of my physical appearance.

For years previously, I had suspected as much. There were too many glances at second helpings, too many sideways opinions and comments about my clothing and the way other people, even strangers, presented themselves to the world.

"That which shalt not be named" had been named, out loud, with actual words that my ears heard. No more reading between the lines. They thought I was overweight. Mortified, I left the kitchen table crying.

I'll have you know that never in my entire childhood was I overweight. There are pictures to prove it: I was a normal kid, a normal kid who never asked to care about her weight. But the weight became everything. And how.

I wasn't about to disagree with their claim that more physical education should happen. I was an orchestra dork who didn't care for sports a bit. Not only that, but as a cellist, I needed a chair to practice my instrument. This meant a good portion of each day was spent practicing while sitting. I was not inclined to go jumping and running around.

Maybe my parents had a point. Still, the point hurt.

These conversations would happen at about the frequency of a typical report card. So by the time I was a senior in high school, I began to anticipate the "buts" at the end of these conversational report cards. There was always a "but." I dreaded the "but." I loathed the "but."

Over time these conversations would get more volatile because with the addition of each new "but" to my arsenal, I was preparing rebuttals for our inevitable forthcoming report card conversations. Also, let's be honest, a roller coaster of hormones was now involved too. With each kitchen table talk, I was progressively more and more prepared for the "but."

"You're doing a great job with your biology projects,
... But we're worried your diet isn't healthy enough.
... But we're worried you're eating too much."

"Your cello concerto is coming along so nicely,
... But we think your weight will keep you from getting a job as a musician.
... But it's a tough world out there and the thinner girl will always get picked for the job."

"Your friends are really wonderful,
... But we're concerned you don't have a boyfriend.
... But we're worried if you get too overweight, no one will want to marry you."

"We know this is hard to hear,
... But we know no one else will tell you this.
... But family is the only source of truth and tough love."

When it comes to Bare Naked Bravery, our external constraints are hard, if not, impossible to control.

When it comes to being a kid in our family, parents are a force to be reckoned with and respected. The two people sitting across the kitchen table were a unified, Texas-sized weather front—impossible to ignore, impossible to stop, impossible to prevent.

Each time we would convene for our seasonal verbal report card, I knew the words that would come out of their mouths would crush my heart for the zillionth time. It happened before. It might hurt worse this time around, if that was even possible. In a lot of these instances, I was not allowed to leave the table. So I would hold on to the previous points of contention in one hand and my prepared rebuttals in the other.

I can't remember each conversation separately. Our kitchen table talks blurred together and got buried deep in the recesses of my brain. If memory had terrain, these conversations would be like the mountains of Nepal. Dark, sharp, icy cold, and with a dangerously suffocating lack of oxygen. Not many people choose to "frolic about" on the ice up there.

However, I do remember one of the first and the more important of these conversations, especially in regards to bravery and using your courage in creative ways.

When I look back, I can see bravery manages to exist in the midst of a less than ideal environment...

It happened while our family was living in France. Sounds fancy, right? For the most part, it was.

Dad was teaching a semester abroad at a university there. By this point, I had been out of public school for a year. The freedom of homeschooling allowed Mom and Dad to bring us along for the adventure.

So hilariously (drum roll please ...) we jumped at this chance of homeschooling freedom to enroll me and my younger sisters in French public school! We would spend our time abroad learning French, cold-turkey, immersion-style. My internal pep-talk went something like, "I know you hated American junior high, but what the heck, let's see if any of that distaste changes with a baguette and brie for lunch."

Mom's pep-talk sounded like, "What an adventure! Isn't that a great idea? Doesn't that seem like so much fun?"

On my first day of French public school, a representative of Dad's hosting university joined my mom and me at the principal's office to help us translate...

[In French]

"Yes, she is from the US.
Yes, Texas.
Yes, Cowboys.
No, she doesn't speak a lick of French.
Yes, we know she's a year older than the other kids in that grade.

No, she doesn't care that she will fail that science class.

Yes, she's just here to learn the language.

Yes, she knows how to walk home from school.

Yes, she has an English-French dictionary.

No, she was not expecting to start today, but I guess she *could*..."

So off I went and wouldn't you know, the first class on my schedule was P.E.

Get this: My first act as an expatriated, formerly homeschooled, appearance-obsessed, middle school student in the French public school system was ...

to take off my clothes in the locker room, in front of my brand-new stranger classmates, whom I had not met yet, whose language I did not speak, whose names I could not pronounce, who because of foreign educational differences were a year behind in age and therefore physical development from me, who were also getting naked like it was no big deal, who were thoroughly intrigued by the fact that I was an American.

Correction: a naked American. A more developed, older, naked American.

It was France. There was a lot of nudity. No surprise, they were okay with me being naked and a stranger. One girl knew enough English to do some rough translation while I stripped down to my skivvies. She wanted immediate confirmation that I drank a glass of milk with my meals just like Rachel and Ross from Friends on television. Their giggly response to my positive confirmation of this dinner tradition made me question the entirety of my personal beverage choices while donning school-issued gym clothes that didn't quite fit and made me super conscious of the curves I never asked for and was reprimanded for at home.

I was beyond grateful my nudity wasn't such a big deal to them. It made the rest of the week a little easier, despite that it was fraught with fearful and vulnerable moments like getting lost in what turned out to be the wrong building and not knowing how to ask for directions.

But I would learn French! What an adventure! Wouldn't that be fun?

In the French education and work culture, everyone gets a glorious two hours for lunch. No surprise, our family chose to do-as-the-French-do, so lunch was our big family meal of the day. Oh the baguettes! Oh the cheese! Oh the glorious cuisine! Finally a culture that understood what it meant to take pleasure in the senses! The French got it.

About two months into our time there I commented on this particular cultural realization at our family lunch. Rather than meeting it with the agreement and similar admiration of the French culture and cuisine that I was expecting, instead the family-wide topic of my diet, my weight, and my exercise habits slapped me in the face and landed on the table next to the baguette.

Our quaint family lunch conversation exploded. And I mean *exploded* all over the walls. My little sisters ran out of the room crying. I was crying, and seething, and could feel my already crumbling sense of belonging falling around my feet. With the mental strength of a fifteen year old, I was doing my darnedest to hold it all together.

"How could they sit there and tell me these things? Here of all places! Don't they know I already know? Yes, they think I'm fat. I hear it in their tone of voice almost every day. Yes, I know what they think about my eating habits."

What I didn't have the words for at the time was this: Don't they know I already feel out of place? I was grappling with the stress of not fitting into my cultural surroundings, my educational surroundings, my geographical surroundings, my linguistic surroundings and here I was sitting at the dinner table with my family in our "home away from home" listening to them tell me I didn't belong there either.

The message was received. Loud and clear. I was eating too much. I wasn't getting enough exercise. I was too fat. I was crying too much. I was yelling too much. I simply was too much.

The undercurrent of not belonging was irrefutable.

The external constraints of my nationality were squeezing my expression dry. The external constraints of being so far away from friends meant there was no one to turn to for consolation. The external constraint of family meant my little sisters were too young to understand. The external constraint of our weird little French apartment mean I slept in the living room, so didn't have a physical place to escape to inside the building. The internal constraints placed on myself were these very valid feelings of loneliness, fear, anger, and tiny belief that "maybe they were right?"

Our bodies and psyches have an uncanny way to finding relief in even the craziest, most constraining and least ideal situations. With this conversation in particular, there was a moment wherein I felt myself float up to the ceiling and must've blacked out from an over-active burst of teenage adrenal hormones, because the next thing I remember is sitting on a bench in a nearby public park.

Relief from the constraints is inevitable. Ask any rubber band.

My escape of the house left me with 30 minutes before school was back in session that afternoon. So in early March, in a foreign country, in a public park, in a mess of tears, bundled up on a bench, I began to tearfully write a letter to a friend back in the States. The little old French ladies walking their dogs in that park thought I was crazy. I could hear their concerned mutterings in my direction.

Crying and writing. Crying and writing. Crying and writing.

I never sent that letter.

Instead I came out of that writing session in the park with a plan, a very cold nose, and almost frozen cheeks. It was early March after all so it was similar to a not-so-funny version of that one scene in the movie "Dumb and Dumber" where Jim Carey's snot freezes to his face. But I had arrived at a solution, gosh darn-it.

My plan was this: If I conceded to my parents' demands and promised to lose 20 lbs before we returned to the States, maybe then they would finally let me pierce my ears for the second time. (Give me a break: I was 15.) Those were my bargaining chips. That's the thing I wanted but knew I couldn't have.

So with the diplomacy of the American-French ambassador and the beady-eyed resolve of our Texas governor at the time, I pulled myself together and gingerly brought the plan back to mom and dad. They hesitated, but approved. We shook hands. I would lose 20 pounds in our final 45 days in France.

My memories of the rest of our time there aren't too strong. I didn't make a lot of friends. I read all 27 English novels from our little town's public library and I spent my lunch hours doing a lot of walking. Because it was France, where every village has a castle, our local castle grounds were maintained as a public park.

I walked those paths for at least an hour every day. Over and over. Some days skipping lunch altogether. It worked. Once a week my walks would take me to the neighborhood pharmacy to use their scale with the large digital numbers and a loud beep with each measurement. The lady pharmacist was impressed but somewhat concerned for the little American teenager who just unnecessarily lost 20 pounds. We smiled politely each time and she would give a lighthearted cheer when the digital numbers announced that my effort was successful.

A couple of weeks before we returned to the US, my ears were pierced. I returned home valiant and 20 pounds lighter.

As I zoom out from that story, on the other side of an eating disorder, it makes me sick to my stomach and leaves a lot of questions.

My parents have their own side of the story, I'm sure of it. Raising a teenager is really tough and I can't imagine any of these moments were enjoyable for them either. Though this certainly never excuses a parent's behavior, it might explain it: My parents, like all parents who try their best, had their own set of constraints—parents have budgets, parents have dreams, parents want to protect their children from how cruel the rest of the world is, parents have their own imperfect parents.

Even in the midst of these moments of volatile constraints, I know mom and dad loved and still love me and I hope they know I loved and still love them. Our family has had to reconcile these events without the promise of definitive answers—at least not the answers any of us would hope for.

But that's the way Bravery (and forgiveness) sometimes looks: unresolved. Eva Cassidy sings, "Time is a healer" and I'll go one step further to also say time is an informer, too. So even though forgiveness cannot tie up all the answers with a beautifully thin bow, over time a practice of building Bravery has highlighted a few nuggets of truth from those days.

Most specifically, when we look back on times of great fear and threatening constraints, moments we thought were cowardice, weakness, and surrender might actually be bravery.

In fact, these moments might be the displays of our greatest Bravery.

Bravery is raising the volume of the conversation to a full blown argument as quickly as possible to make sure your little sisters run out of the room to get away from the back splash of painful words.

Bravery is staring at a baguette like your life depended on it. Anything to avoid possessing the memory of their face saying *those* words. Bravery is then magically floating up to the ceiling and 'blacking out' to forget the pain of every word. Maybe this shows unmistakable resilience to lose parts of memory to emotional trauma.

Bravery is finding a safe place to express yourself, somewhere, anywhere. It is writing a letter to a friend when she's literally half a world away, even if you're not sure you'll actually send it.

It might not've been ideal, but my bravery flirted with grave danger to trade it for the lesser of two evils. I negotiated emotional distance from "You don't belong." by transforming it into "You can get what you want."

I certainly didn't know I was doing all that. How could I? I was 15, I was in the throes of hormones. Yet somehow, Bare Naked Bravery knows how to find the resources available and make creative use of them.

We are a resourceful breed, us humans. It might take decades to recognize the brilliance found in the really dark places, but somewhere even in the midst of it, our Bravery makes a way for us, even when the tears prevent us from seeing straight.

We hear stories proving this all over history.

In art history books you'll find that a trolley accident left Frida Kahlo with a life of pain and suffering. But she still managed to make emblematic art, become a beacon of feminine strength, and evoke a deep sense of national pride even in the midst of a terribly tumultuous love affair.

In psychiatry you'll hear of Victor Frankl, a socialist Viennese psychiatrist and neurologist who experienced the inside of multiple concentration camps, one of which was Auschwitz. After surviving the Holocaust he used this experience to form what we now call Logotherapy which is founded upon the belief that it's the striving to find meaning in one's life that is the primary, most powerful motivating and driving force in humans. To come full circle on his own story, logotherapy is now one of the treatments for substance abuse as a result of military-related PTSD.

In researching and observing bravery in the people around me and throughout history, I've seen there are three types of bravery. Knowing these has made the process of "being brave" so much easier because according to the situation I'm facing, I'm able to narrow down exactly how the bravery should show up in the world, therefore informing me in turn how I should show up in the world.

The 3 Forms of Bravery & How to Find Fairy Godmothers

We are products of our environments. A long line of catastrophic thinkers, perfectionists, and serious analytic personalities make up my heritage— each with his or her own deeply set value systems. Collectively we are Eagle Scouts, ER nurses, advertising executives, Marines, Air Force pilots, engineers, grammar teachers, dentists, and piano teachers. We are world-traveling Swedish/Irish/ Scottish Immigrants and longtime natives of Kentucky, Michigan, California, and Georgia.

Last time I visited my California counterparts they lovingly cajoled me into a spontaneous "two-song performance" after dinner. A West Coast house concert tour had brought me through town, so I already had my instruments stashed in the house. This made turning down their request a hard thing to do. My little cousins are particularly cute and my aunts are, well, let's just say very convincing.

What I was not expecting was for those two songs to turn into a full sing-along-request-hour-with-Cousin-Emily-Ann. We started with favorites from Sound of Music and then somehow it ended with a finale of The National Anthem, at which point everyone in the living room stood up and put their right hand over their heart. Did I mention we're proud Americans?

My family loves to plan ahead, almost to a fault. A couple years ago, my Eagle Scout, Army-Ranger-turned-Professor father connected his university to the nonprofit indie rock band I was in at the time. Quite a pairing huh?

Social justice awareness concerts were my band's schtick, so it made a lot of sense to be hosted by universities. We loved it. So on tour one season, all six of us bandmates traveled cross-country to perform for my dad's university. Before we even set foot in the door of my parents' house to shake off the travel dust, dad welcomed us on the front lawn by handing us each a sheet of paper, single-spaced, size 12 font.

I saw my bandmates' eyes widen. There we stood with a detailed itinerary of our entire three-day weekend, segmented into 15-minute increments. Looking at this well-documented itinerary struck pride in my chest (after all I am my father's daughter—I didn't fall far from the tree.) But a big ol' knot in my stomach began to swell. I had forgotten to adequately warn my bandmates about my family. I had also failed to remind my dad that almost half of the band was from Hawaii and therefore abide by "Island Time" regardless of which US state we were in.

According to our itinerary, eating sandwiches was going to take 30 minutes and waking up at 9am would take 15 minutes. Ha! Little did he know. It all worked out in the end, but needless to say, it was a weekend to remember—which I was sure to mention at my father's "debriefing meeting" at the 09:00 on the last day of that weekend. I love my dad.

Not only do we love to plan ahead for things, but my family tends to assume the worst and somehow get a total kick out of being prepared for it. My aunt, cousin, and I giggle with glee over our shared catastrophic thinking during plane takeoffs. Of course we *know* nothing is likely to happen, but we simply can't help it. We joke about "what might happen" on road trips and scheme our route of escape should the logger truck in front of us suddenly lose its grip on the massive logs traveling at 70 mph down the Georgia freeway.

Maybe we do this because multiple layers of pioneer make up the blood that pumps through our veins: Swedish, Irish, Scottish, and Kentuckian. I'm proud to have this brave genealogy and generous take-no-bullshit upbringing. To this day, those two things support me quite sufficiently when I'm faced with my biggest constraints. It's as if my great-great-great-great grandparents reach through the folds of time to give me extra doses of perseverance when persevering is the very last thing I think I can do.

Did I mention I grew up in the South? Southern women, my family especially, are some of the strongest, most generous, get-things-done group of humans I know. Consequently Southern women are also the most bullheaded group of humans I know.

Contrary to medical research, it is my strong belief that the amount of butter Southern women put in their recipes has something to do with lubricating the sheer amount of heroism pulsing through their veins.

As with any sparkly and bright upbringing there is an equally matte and dark side. It's not all roses, sunshine, and sweet tea. Everyone's parents and heritage have failed us some way or another. Growing up around Southern women taught me to admire hospitality, pay attention to small details, and connect with my surrounding community. From these same take-no-bullshit women, I also ironically learned ...

... to master the perfection of appearances.

... to put others first at all costs, even at the cost of self.

... to throw myself under the bus.

Add my previously mentioned deep-set value system, catastrophic and analytic thinking into that mix and the pressure eventually caused the internal structure of my worldview to crumble into dust. Eventually I also crumbled into dust as fine as the powdered sugar sprinkled on the tea cakes sitting in front of me at brunch—the same tea cakes I was taught to kindly refuse lest my dress size reflect my "too-muchness."

The fears of failure, abandonment, shame, pain, and being "too much" were real. They were too real. At least, too real for my full comprehension at the time.

By the time I was a 17, my Southern education in perfect appearances paid off in a full blown graduate degree in eating disorders from the School of Hard Knocks. I found myself severely abusing laxatives. First a couple of pills at a time and then eventually a fistful each day, sometimes multiple times each day. I exercised brutally hard for up to five hours at a time, and ate practically nothing for the majority of my senior year of high school.

Crumbling on the inside yet oh so perfectly coiffed on the outside, I was fighting my internal emotions and related constraints just as hard as I was exercising, which was a lot. I lost 40 pounds in less than two months.

To put my cultural surroundings in further perspective, at my most extreme, my drastic weight loss merely signaled to my family that after years of their encouragement to lose weight, something was finally working. Huzzah! Hiding imperfections was now a specialty of mine as well, I should be proud. Or at least that's what I told myself.

I wouldn't wish mental illness, any mental illness, on even my worst enemy. Talk about inhumane torture. There are still moments when my skin crawls with the memories of using fear and constraints in those ways. Catch me on a good day and I'll still have a hard time being in the presence of someone who reminds me of that time.

You can bet your butt that there was a season when I blamed my family (the whole lot of them) for everything I went through. I blamed them with the full gusto of all the Southern women that could fit in a Super Walmart. That's a lot of blame and a lot of bullheaded women.

> Side-note: An unintentional side effect of building Bare Naked Bravery, is that bravery gets easier. In this case, forgiveness of myself came easier and therefore forgiveness of my family comes easier too. The practices mentioned later in this book led me far from a state of blame and pointing fingers. I do not blame them any longer. I can see my parents were unfortunately living and loving according to what was laid before them.

On the surface, I was doing "Just beautifully!" but inside I was melting from the pressure of keeping up appearances. My life was crumbling on the inside. The outside followed soon after.

Using the same willpower and militaristic fortitude of my voluntary hunger strikes and exercise sessions, I had managed to swear off the laxative abuse. This choice had nothing to do with the threat of having a heart attack at the ripe age of 21 nor did it have anything to do with the notion of permanently ruining my intestinal tract.

I vainly swore laxatives off because there were one too many 'close calls' to the restroom. Laxative abuse was inconvenient. It was getting harder and harder to hide the pills' side-effects of sheer urgency to get to a bathroom. (Appearances, remember?)

So one fateful day, a year into my battle of will-power against laxatives, I found myself walking up the stairwell to my dorm. I looked down at my hand. Under my thumb was a brand new box of laxatives and its receipt. For the life of me, I don't remember buying them, and yet, there they were.

Internal Bravery

It was as if my compulsion had taken me hostage and then went on a joyride to Walgreens to buy only laxatives. Normally, I would buy some snacks, some lady products, and a bottle of nail polish to "hide" the purchase of my laxatives. According to the receipt, I had totally blacked out during this joy ride because I didn't even have the decency to buy other things along with them! What must the cashier have thought of me?! (Appearances, remember?)

Standing on the stairwell balcony, I knew I had a seriously scary problem. If I couldn't keep up my appearances with a pharmacy clerk, then it was out of control and I was out of control, no longer able to take charge of the crisis. Facing this truth required all the Internal Bravery I could muster.

I knew the stakes were high. I knew learning how to swim during a hurricane is not a good idea. Neither is the idea of exploring new communication techniques during a fight, about your marriage, with your wife. Nor is it a good idea to acquire a new painting technique while restoring a Monet. The stakes are way too high. The margin of error and external standards in those situations are astronomically high, which means the likelihood of taking new risks and being successful is astronomically low. Continuing to face this eating disorder on my own was not a good idea.

Recognizing these moments of Internal Bravery in your story is powerful. What I know now is that internal bravery is subjective. It is secret to only the person being brave. Internal bravery exists when in the midst of depression I find the strength to put on pants and take myself to the store for groceries. I'm the only one in that grocery store who knows that I'm being brave in that moment.

In talking with so many people about bravery, I've heard stories of their own internal bravery: The moment she knew beyond a shadow of a doubt that divorce was inevitable. The strength it took to press "send" on that first email to a new client. The act of putting that box of tattered mementos in the trash. The act of licking the stamp and dropping the anonymous witness statement to the police.

When you overhear yourself randomly think "Oh how I need to quit my job." that's internal bravery. When you take a deep breath before walking into the party that your ex is also likely to attend. When your journal pages hold the first utterance of how tormented your relationship makes you. When your boss unintentionally or intentionally makes you feel as small as a cricket, but you tell yourself "Good job" regardless. When you stealthily change the subject to avoid that *other* subject at the party.

For me, that night, Internal Bravery was in full effect. There were mental sirens wailing and red lights flashing in my head. Simply adding another green smoothie to my diet was not going to fix this mother cluster.

"I thought I had a grip on this thing. I thought I could get myself out of this literal shit show," I said while looking at the laxative receipt.

Beaming my willpower in its direction wasn't making it all go away. It was getting too messy trying to keep up the charade of running from this monstrous mental illness. Keeping up appearances was demanding and terrifying. Clearly my methods of managing it all were not working because here I was again under the spell of a package of laxatives falsely promising to rid me of all my problems.

We'll talk about this later, but acknowledging when you're facing a moment of internal bravery automatically puts the power of choice back into your hands. Regardless of the situation, hearing yourself acknowledge the courage you're secretly displaying is what gives you more power to choose whether you want to stretch the bravery beyond its internal boundaries.

External Bravery

That's what happened that day on the stairwell in my dorm. I admitted to myself that something had to change. But if this deadly cycle of succumbing and regaining control was to break, I knew I would need help. Managing crisis after crisis like this was not living. Death was staring me squarely in the eyes and seductively breathing down my neck.

I called Cassandra—a friend, a saint, and fellow eating disorder sinner. She was someone who knew what it was like to manage a sinking ship like mine. She would be able to help because as it turned out, Cassandra and I both bobbed and weaved through the anorexic/bulimic dance of college life. We had confessed our respective eating disorders to each other after our study group for the semester final for Food & Nutrition college class. (The irony is not lost on me.)

The minute we invite or involve someone else into bravery AND when they know you're being brave too, that's external bravery. Confessing to your best friend about your inevitable divorce, that's external bravery. Inviting your family members over to talk about your hoarding problem, that's external bravery. Calling the addiction rehab facility, that's external bravery. Walking through the door to have breakfast with someone you haven't seen in 20 years, that's external bravery.

For that night, calling Cassandra was my act of external bravery.

When Cassandra picked up the phone, I sank to my knees in the dorm stairwell. All that came out of my mouth was incomprehensible mutterings, sobs, and the sound of snot evacuating my face. Without saying anything, I knew she was on her way over. She stayed on the phone while driving to the dorm. She stayed on the phone while I made my way inside, wracked in fear and disgust. She let herself in and found me full-body crying into the carpet. Together we left a message with the campus doctor for the following day. We both cried until there were no more tears. I could hear her leave soon as I drifted to sleep after exhausting my carpet's capacity for collecting tears. I slept that night on the floor.

Finding Fairy Godmothers

It turns out Cassandra was a fairy godmother, even though I was unaware such a magical visit was occurring. Fairy Godmothers don't wear full-length, pink, glittery gowns with a tiara anymore. In fact, I think several of them wear crew socks with sandals or frequently walk around with lipstick on their teeth. They aren't glamorous. But they are good. So good.

The next day was my first obvious visit from a fairy godmother. This particular fairy godmother wore a white coat and held a clipboard while very clearly telling me I did "not have to live like this." She diagnosed me with an eating disorder (duh) and helped me take the next steps to collect a team of professional fairy godmothers: a nutritionist, a specialized medical doctor, and a therapist. Together we began to understand and unwrap the cluster fuck under which I was suffocating.

Eventually I found the perfect fit in a therapist. A therapist who saw me from a new angle, who challenged me by gently asking the tough questions. He had professional experience with similar stories to mine. He was willing to stick it out through the long haul and not just shove a stack of scriptures into my hands and expect me to just "pray it away." (Something I experienced more than once during my recovery.) I needed him to remind me of the important things, like "You know, life doesn't have to be this hard. You can always ask for more help. You don't have to do this alone."

You see, we need the experts' opinion to see our own progress. We need the advice of fairy godfathers. We need their encouragement. We need their heroism. We need someone to ask the hard questions. We need the boundaries of their professionalism to know we're not a 'burden.' We need their knowledge and experience on our side. We need to trust someone to give us the right kind of nudge in the right direction.

We need the pioneering declarations that only fairy godmothers can make. They give us the permission to do the things we had always hoped we could do when we don't have the life-capacity nor the capability to give ourselves the permission.

Fairy godmothers swoop in and give us the extra $50 to take that one class, even when we could've paid for it ourselves (but definitely weren't going to.) They listen to the whole song without stopping to comment and then challenge you to your next creative endeavor. Unprompted, they send you a more professional microphone in the mail after hearing your first attempts to record original music.

Get as many fairy godmothers and godfathers as you can. Find your favorites. Spend as much time as you can with them. Make playlists of the pros. Listen to them on repeat until your ears bleed and you have the words and cadence memorized. Become the world's sneakiest fairy godmother copy cat. Take lessons with them. Often. Let them melt your brain with their genius, brilliance and expertise until it's mush. Read their books. Read their memoirs. Read their history. Answer their tough questions. Observe their Bare Naked Bravery.

Even if your bravery bucket is as dry as the desert, sponge it up, every drop you find. Eventually the bravery will ooze out of you too, whether you like it or not.

Maybe your fairy godmother just responded to an email with, "Umm ... why didn't you tell me you were a writer?!" Maybe another is a grade school art teacher. High school English teacher. Grandparent. Aunt. Favorite author. Uncle. Celebrity. Parent. Therapist. Random person at last week's wine and cheese night.

Whoever it is, they whisper in our ears "Be you! Go! Do! Make! It's worth it!"

We really do need fairy godmothers. Otherwise, we'd go around with spinach in our teeth making epically poor decisions. We need them because sometimes we cannot find a safe place for ourselves without their assistance. We need them because we need their Bare Naked Bravery.

Resonant Bravery

Along my recovery story and throughout the rest of this unquenchable curiosity for "What is bravery?" I discovered a third form: Resonant Bravery.

Whenever I heard someone or witnessed someone else do something brave, I too became just a little bit braver. Whenever the goosebumps popped up on my skin while witnessing someone do something I could only dream of doing myself, I encountered Resonant Bravery.

When Obama became the first black president of the United States, among other things I felt Resonant Bravery. When we hear stories of people breaking stereotypes and busting through cultural stigmas, we feel Resonant Bravery. When we watch someone overcome seemingly insurmountable odds to achieve something, we feel Resonant Bravery.

Here's my favorite part of Resonant Bravery: The person doing "the brave thing" does not need to know nor feel that they are brave. Like beauty, Resonant Bravery is subjective.

When I watch an attorney give her closing statement, even though this is something she does almost every day, I'm still captivated by Resonant Bravery. When I watch someone stop to help someone else in need, even if that's by doing something they don't think is brave at all, that's still Resonant Bravery. It's Resonant Bravery because *I* think it's a brave thing to do.

On a lighter note, when a bold audacious comedian posts a picture of herself in a bikini on social media and people begin to leave comments like "That's so brave!" What they really mean is, "Wow, if I did something like that, I'd be doing something really brave." Posting scandalous or viral pictures is not necessarily a brave thing for Amy Schumer, Chelsea Handler, or any other boundary-busting human to do. But it does inspire Resonant Bravery in others.

This is exactly why we need *your* bravery. We need you to get out there and stand up, show up, speak up because it will inevitably inspire one of us to stand up, show up, speak up in a way that only we can.

I recently attended a music conference with a bunch of folk musicians. On the first morning of the weekend-long conference, I decided to join a friend and attend a panel discussion titled "Everybody can make a record. Nobody can make a living. Now what?"

I really wish I had read the panel description more clearly, because I soon found out this panel turned into an hourlong discussion about what wasn't working in the industry. There's a lot of negativity in the world already. There's a lot of negativity in the music industry already. I was *really* not in the mood to continue listening to what wasn't working. I summoned up some internal bravery to walk out of the room before the discussion completed.

While quietly gathering my things I turned to my friend sitting next to me and blurted out some external bravery, "I'm actually really *excited* about where the industry is going and the way this conversation is headed is making me unnecessarily depressed. I'm gonna leave and be out in the foyer."

She convinced me to stay with her own version of external bravery and responded with, "Then say so! Stay! Speak up."

So I did. I raised my hand and waited my turn add to the discussion. When called upon I said, "I disagree."

The panel moderator paused, bewildered by the sudden difference of opinion, "You disagree with what?"

"I disagree with everything. I'm really excited about the potential that we all have in our industry. Never in the history of being a musician has it been easier to share music with our audiences. Technology has not cursed us, it has empowered us."

What followed in that panel was a total 180 degree flip. The other attendees who were visibly concerned and vocally discouraged were now curious. The panel moderator was visibly flustered by the sharp turn of subject matter. The handful of attendees who were in agreement with a sense of optimism began to raise their hands in agreement, adding to the excitement.

In this instance, my internal bravery to leave the room early caused my friend to be externally brave by asking me to stay and speak up. This caused a ripple effect of Resonant Bravery through countless conversations of agreement and curiosity with other attendees that day and throughout the rest of the weekend. There were even a handful of strangers who simply thanked me for speaking up. This ripple effect of Resonant Bravery is *still* going, because here I am putting the story in a book for you to read. If you later have a conversation with a friend or colleague about this, then you'll be passing on the Resonant Bravery even further.

I laugh because it all started with my own internal bravery to sneak out of the conversation completely.

Why We Do Brave Things

I don't know why horrific things happen. I don't know why random acts of trauma happen. I'm okay with not fully knowing the answer. No one's pretending that I'm a grief counselor, or a therapist, or a philosopher. I don't have acronyms after my last name. People don't call me Dr. Peterson, that's my dad. But I am a songwriter. I do have eyes and ears. I know how to listen to stories and pass them on and I'm not scared of dark places. I've done a lot of living in those dark places. There are parts of life that, to me, will remain a mystery and I'm okay with that.

But I do know this: when bad things happen there is always bravery nearby. During tragic events the beloved Fred Rogers' own mother is famous for saying, "Look for the helpers. There are always helpers." Same goes for bravery. Look for the bravery. There is always bravery.

In the midst of what may seem like total chaos in our world are glimmers of hope. We can look inside ourselves and see the seeds of our Internal Bravery floating throughout our days. We can see the seeds of External Bravery between ourselves and our lovers or friends. We can feel the effects of Resonant Bravery ripple throughout our communities and culture.

So if I can't answer the question, "Why do bad things happen?" then I *can* answer, "Why do we do brave things?" The pursuit of "why" helps us discover the "what." Here's what I've noticed about the reasons behind feats of bravery.

People do brave things for three reasons

1. Bravery is contagious.
2. The thing on the other side of the feat of bravery is worth the discomfort.
3. Someone else needs us to be brave.

Reason 1: Because It's Contagious.

I touched a little on this concept at TEDxTacoma in 2014. You'd never know it by watching the video of my talk, but that day as I walked across the stage with its signature red accents, my world was crashing around my ankles. I had been officially diagnosed with my hand tremor just a couple weeks prior.

Despite the medication I was prescribed, a tiny hint of the tremor survived that day. If you watch the talk, at certain moments you can see it while I nervously switch hands to hold my shaking note cards with a more stable hand. I wish I hadn't used those note cards. I truly know this stuff like the back of my shaking hand. I was just battling stage fright and high expectations and the rest of the massive amount of uncertainty in my life.

Without giving you the talk again here in written form, let me just say that the ripple effect of shared experiences is unlimited. The potential to find value in each other as humans is so vast and innumerable, that we've created elaborate systems to represent the exchange of this value.

There is SO much potential for good in the world, especially in light of this knowledge, that this potential for good spreads. In fact, the more we share experiences with each other, the more that value is duplicated and the more it can grow exponentially. Think about this: being inspired by the people around you, causes you to think, behave, and act out of a similar mode of inspiration. That inspiration, when practiced enough, will unintentionally cause other people around you to do the same and that process goes on without end.

One morning, after writing the memoir portions of this book, I started the research of the writing process by opening social media and perusing the list of my personal friends. Who among them was brave? Who did I know personally to be truly brave?

Within 20 minutes I filled one side of an 8.5x11 sheet of paper with names. So many friends, family, and colleagues who I thought were courageous. There are so many of them doing amazing things in big or small ways.

Big ways: starting schools, quitting jobs, getting pregnant after losing the first, second, and third baby, battling cancer, living overseas, starting nonprofits...

Small ways: calling me on my shit, calling me when they suspected I needed help, openingly sharing unique perspectives, creating something and putting it out into the world, never giving up...

Staring at that piece of paper with 50-plus names of friends, family, and colleagues, I had to take a deep breath. It was so obvious. In that moment, bravery became this pulsating, swirling part of the atmosphere. Except, unlike oxygen and carbon dioxide, when we "breathe" in bravery, it just creates more bravery. It creates more bravery inside ourselves. It creates more bravery externally, and therefore more bravery in other people too through the resonance of life. We'll unfold more on resonance later.

Today, I see the contagious effects of bravery in a tangible way with the Bare Naked Bravery podcast. At the end of every interview recording, my guests get a chance to nominate someone they know personally to appear on the show. Those nominees are invited to speak on future shows. Since the show has been around for awhile, today I find myself interviewing people on the sixth, seventh or eighth degrees of separation from members of that original list.

Becoming Conscious of Our Bravery

The more conscious you are about the existence of bravery and its ingredients, the more of them you have.

Here's one of the favorite things I've learned about neurology in the last couple years. Stay with me. It's worth it.

Every neuron in our brain is connected to other neurons through synapses. Whenever we do or think something, we're pulsing energy or electricity through specific synapses. If we're doing something we've never done before, the connection between those synapses is not as strong as the connections between synapses that have fired countless times.

Let's try something: with your dominant hand, typically the hand you write with, rub your nose. Put your hand back where it was. Now repeat that 5 separate times while noticing how easy it is to rub your nose. Now with the pinky of your other hand, your non-dominant hand, rub the opposing ear. This will either be your left pinky finger scratching your right ear or right pinky finger scratching your left ear. Put your hand back where it was. Repeat that 2 more times while noticing how totally weird it feels.

Here's my favorite part: Now do that simple movement with your non dominant hand 5 times while noticing how much easier it feels. I bet if you did that action 10 times, it'd feel pretty damn comfy too.

As we repeat these new actions, thoughts, and behaviors, those new connections between synapses get stronger through strengthening of this thing called myelin around each connection. I like to think of myelin as tiny, long, sticky pieces of tape wrapped around and around the synapses we practice the most.

This myelin is created through repetition of a behavior, act, or thought. The more we repeat something, the more myelin gets wrapped around the synapses required to accomplish the repetition. In turn, those synapses are stronger and easier for our brain to access.

Scratching your ear with the "wrong" finger or hand is a great example of this. But so is playing an instrument. Successfully playing a particular set of fingerings and bowings just once might be extremely difficult. But successfully repeating this same difficult passage of music 10 or more times in a row, automatically implies that this same passage is now exponentially easier. (Thanks myelin!) After 10 repetitions, perhaps the passage of music is not the easiest it will ever be, but it's still easier.

What does this have to do with Bravery and how we make more Bravery by being more aware of it?

Repetition of any task (including thoughts about and surrounding bravery) builds myelin around the synapses required to do that task. The more myelin there is between synapses, the easier it is to repeat that task, thought, or behavior.

When it comes to pro-active knowledge and discovery of Bravery, we are metaphorically breathing the bravery in, creating more of it because those thought and behavior patterns are getting reinforced with more myelin. This is partly what contributes to the cyclical nature of creativity and courage.

Consciousness of bravery begets more bravery. So we need your bravery because the more bravery *we* see, the more we are conscious of it. The more we are conscious of it, the more myelin gets wrapped around those "bravery synapses." The more those synapses are strengthened, the easier it is for us to be brave.

So in essence, we are brave because the bravery surrounding us inspires us to be brave.

Reason 2: Because It's Worth It.

When the grass on the other side of the fence is greener than your own stinky, brown, messy lawn, hoisting your leg up over that fence and hefting yourself over is worth it.

Truly, this happens all the time in the sales world. Infomercials are effective, albeit sometimes ridiculous, when they highlight how bad things are right now (fumbling around and dropping your keys like they're covered in butter) and how amazing life is going to be (with the new key/phone/wallet invention of the year) once you do the a painful thing (forking over the dough to pay) and receive this life-changing product.

We do uncomfortable things all the time because it's worth it. Things like admitting you're sorry/wrong so you can maintain peace in the household, learning how to cook to woo a first date, trapeze lessons so we can almost-fly, chores so the house looks decent for company.

A similar thing happens with bravery. Sometimes we do the brave thing not just because it's contagious, but because we know the discomfort of being brave will be worth it.

Reason 3: Because It's Needed.

"There are still many causes worth sacrificing for, so much history yet to be made."—Michelle Obama

The third and sometimes most effective reason people do brave things is because that act of bravery is needed by someone else. People jump into burning buildings and do really crazy stuff just because someone is on the other side who needs their help.

My favorite example of this is a viral video titled "Aussiest. Interview. Ever." You can watch the video for yourself in the book bonuses. (Available here: http://emilyannpeterson.com/bnb-book)

For the sake of right now, I'll just say the video cuts to a news reporter holding a microphone to the mouth of this guy with a *very* Aussie accent. He starts going on about how a hit-and-run driver ran his car into a shop owned by his mate's mom. With nothing on but his underwear, he chased the culprit down the road until the cops intercepted.

The news reporter then says, "Well you've managed to put some pants on in the meantime. That's good to hear. Do you feel like a hero?"

"Uh. Not really mate, it's just something you gotta do for the community mate. You look after your mates and your mates'll always look after you."

It truly is the most Australian thing you'll ever see, but exactly like the other newscaster says, "Just goes to show you what you can achieve in your underwear."

That's hilarious and all to think about, running down the street in nothing but briefs because someone needs you to do something brave. But it applies to more than just viral feel-good newscaster videos.

When I talk with my clients and colleagues about self-promotion (a very brave thing to do for a lot of us) we can discuss content creation, product promotion, shaking hands, and marketing campaigns until we're all blue in the face. But for a lot of folks, until we realize how *needed* our bravery is we aren't willing to face the discomfort of actually doing the brave thing. Perhaps this is a poor reflection of our self-worth, but it remains an effective method of "getting over" the fear of putting yourself out there.

This is the same reason people sell all their belongings to go help in refugee camps, start nonprofits or spend hours and hours of precious time away from their families volunteering for noble causes. Sometimes you need to be brave because someone out there needs you to be brave.

Triple Threats

If you're facing something brave or terrifying, one the best ways to overcome avoidance or procrastination or total shell shock of fear is to answer the following questions …

Will this feat inspire bravery in someone else?
What's on the other side of this feat of bravery?
Who needs me to be brave in this way?

Over time, I've noticed that in the moments I'm facing something brave and I'm terrified - answering those three questions reminds me that what I'm about to do is worth it, how it's contagious, and who needs me to do the brave thing. Often, I realize that I've forgotten about one or more of the three reasons. Remembering that second or third reason why I want to be brave makes doing the brave thing that much easier.

Now that you know how creativity and courage rely on each to grow and expand and that bravery can look different when we are forced to be resilient or in less than ideal environments, I want to expound on to the three forms of bravery (internal, external, resonant) and the three reasons bravery happens (because it's contagious, it's worth it, and it's needed.) In the remaining portions of this book we'll dive into the

12 ingredients of bravery. Knowing these ingredients has empowered my own bravery in the last several years. It's such a relief to encounter brave moments and recognize, "This is a job for vulnerability!" and know exactly how to reach for and include more of that ingredient in my life.

Part Two

Vulnerability = Risk + Context + Honesty

"The act of being seen can become one of the most ultimate vulnerabilities of all. Because one of the corollaries of being seen is that you are heard."—David Whyte

Mark Manson, one of my favorite writer/bloggers, describes vulnerability as "consciously choosing not to hide your emotions or desires from others." The beloved Brené Brown describes vulnerability as "emotional exposure." She suggests (and I agree) that you're not being vulnerable unless you're feeling somewhat exposed, figuratively or literally. Sharing crazy experiences, revealing secrets, showing your 'weak spots,' confessing your loyalty or betrayal— depending upon the context, these are the things of strength.

There are three underpinnings of vulnerability as it pertains to bravery: honesty, risk, and context. The context of your vulnerability can sometimes define it. Yet in the end, you are the only one that can determine how that vulnerability presents itself because it requires *your* honesty and the unique risk given each moment.

Let's use a hypothetical scenario as explanation.

In 1997 the song "MMMbop" was at the top of the charts and nominated for three Grammy awards. That year, the act of confessing to being an ardent fan of Hanson was not a vulnerable act of exposure for a teenage girl. Nay, it was a symbol of pride. The cultural context of that year in American pop music could evoke a tribal sense of belonging from the musical confession of being a fan of Hanson.

If this same teenage girl were to take this piece of hypothetical news—that she is a fan of Hanson—and present it to a Hanson fan club's annual meet-up, her confession would neither feel vulnerable internally nor be received as vulnerable externally. The fan club's response would simply be "Duh. Isn't that why you're here?" Because this external context is easier to predict, the choice to reveal her fandom might not be as risky. She will most likely be welcomed with open arms.

But it's a different story, especially if this hypothetical, now grownup teenage girl is a musician living in the centrifugal force of today's hipster music scene. Standing backstage before or after a show in Seattle is not quite as comfortable for former-teeny-boppers-turned-musicians. Hanson's "MMMbop" doesn't do well with six-course farm-to-table meals, artisan coffee roasts, and handmade goods. The context of a confession like this implies quite a bit more social and career risk. She shouldn't expect a hearty reception upon confessing that as a teen she used her kid sisters' sidewalk chalks to semi-permanently graffiti a Hanson logo onto the driveway of their Texas home.

The recipient of this backstage news is also an external factor of this hypothetical vulnerability. The confessor of former fandom has essentially given her colleagues the permission to make a judgment about her "hipster scorecard" and rate the validity of her involvement in the music industry. She cannot control what her colleagues (or the rest of the world) think of her once the musical cat is "MMMbopped" out of the bag. Her confession of Hanson fandom might fall anywhere along a spectrum between "Wow this chick is clearly an avid, longtime lover of pop music," to "This chick has lousy taste in music and doesn't deserve to be on a stage."

The way this confession is received is impossible to accurately predict, because of this there is vulnerability within the confessor. To some, a pro musician confessing this bit of fandom news in a book would certainly be a vulnerable act ... if it weren't hypothetical.

But this my favorite part of vulnerability: In the end, you are the only one that can determine your measure of vulnerability. You always have a choice in how you expose yourself (or not.)

wink

So in light of that freedom of choice let's dive into how risk plays a role in this vulnerability. Knowing this can clear up your choice in *how* you are brave while maintaining the safety you require to move forward in that bravery.

Risk

"If you don't risk anything, you risk even more."—Erica Jong

When shit hits the fan there might not be a wrong or right next step. There is no hard and fast rule about how to encounter your fears. "Feeling the fear and doing it anyway," might not be the answer every time, because do-or-die is not always bravery.

Bravery asks us to listen, to observe, and to move forward. Sometimes it means taking bold risks and sometimes that looks like staying home in your pajamas. Sometimes bravery is choosing to ask, "What does 'forward' look like today?" Bravery is asking us to just keep going within our vulnerability and honesty.

There is a lot of gray area here. I know. I see it too. Sometimes we won't know if we've made an "unsafe," too risky choice, gambling too much potential on unresponsive contexts. Sometimes we won't know if we've exposed ourselves too much until we get a sunburn.

This is where practicing Bravery comes into play. Only fresh, inexperienced tourists to the equator will get second-degree sunburn. More experienced travelers will know how important sunscreen is to the first three days of a visit to the equator. Your experience with exposure can ruin your trip or make it great.

Our risk, our exposure, our vulnerability are not necessarily weakness. Andre Lorde would also add,

"... that visibility which makes us most vulnerable is that which also is the source of our greatest strength."

Going around the corner to get a cup of coffee has few unknowns to a local. It's not a risky trip. It's not new. The dulled vision of this local coffeeshop enthusiast will see the neighborhood cafe as mundane. Everything is same old, same old. The colors of the wall get lost in the monotony of time.

But the fresh eyes of a tourist who's risked the comfort of home can see the same cafe and acknowledge its vibrancy. The fact that tourists are exposed to newness fosters a fresh sense of vision. They've left their comfort zones at home. Something as mundane as going to a cafe two towns away counts for this. You'll see the world in a unique way.

When naivete and exposure are accompanied with risk and newness, we get vulnerability. When this vulnerability is accompanied with improvisation, imagination, and honesty about constraints, we get immense strength and courage.

Our vulnerability is not fragility. Quite the opposite. Vulnerability is strength.

Benefits of Boundaries & Being Bullheaded

My favorite metaphor of creativity/art/expression is the pinecone. To me, it symbolizes fiercely guarding your potential with almost impenetrable surroundings which just so happen to be packed with nutrients for future growth. The seeds inside the pinecone need the external protective layers for nutrients later.

For similar reasons the Sequoia Redwood trees need fire. Forest fires clear the surrounding soil of weeds and other foliage which make room for the huge force of nature of a Sequoia. Not only that, but heat and smoke from the forest fire gets caught under the canopy of mature Redwoods which then opens the pinecone to reveal and release the Redwood seeds.

It takes time and destruction to make a pinecone ready to germinate its seeds. Nature is brilliant and brutally honest. The Redwood is not the only creature on this planet that needs to create a nurturing environment for its future. We need this too.

We can't entrust our tender potential to a boxer wielding an iron fist. We can't propose to someone on a first date without a good chance of that proposal getting declined. We can't take our brand new unhatched indie film concept to just *anyone*. We can't bring new laws, not fully thought through, to the powers at be without them getting shot down. Those personal, relational, cultural, social and legal boundaries exist for a reason!

The boundaries, obstacles, spikes and spurs on that pinecone exist for a reason because protecting potential is a massive part of boundaries and of being brave.

It's okay to gather your safest friends for a season and turn off social media. It's okay to pause a work friendship after getting laid off. It's okay to draw a line with someone to avoid discussing a certain subject matter. It's okay to build those personal boundaries. Just keep in mind that the more boundaries that exist, the harder it is to be seen, the harder it is to share experiences and therefore spread that gorgeous bravery of yours.

Are your boundaries proactive or reactive?

Neither is better than the other. It's just a really great question to ask when you're facing a brave moment and considering crossing or breaking a boundary. Knowing the source and reasoning behind your boundaries can inform your decisions involving bravery.

Since I'm well-practiced in the world of online dating, let's use that as an example. Proactive boundaries might look like purposely not shaving your legs on a first date, so you're less likely to "give it all away" in one go, even though that's never happened before.

Reactive boundaries might look like finally convincing your cell phone provider to block the jerk's number because of his persistently inappropriate texts. Reactive boundaries might come in the form of a restraining order or a cease and desist letter from an attorney.

Is this my boundary or someone else's?

It's not called bravery when our boundaries are pushed, threatened, or torn down by others without our permission. That's called disrespect, rudeness, abuse, and possibly rape—intense, but accurate vocabulary depending on the situation.

I know so many men and women whose boundaries have been disrespected, myself included. It's a horrible feeling. It goes straight to the center of your gut and lands with a sharp and direct thud. Then if it hasn't happened already, every muscle in your body tenses up. Depending on the severity of the violation, it can take years to feel safe enough to let go from those defensive (and appropriate) reactions.

For me, the feeling after a first date gone bad was the same physical tension and gut-level thud as recognizing a business contract was going very bad very fast. The void of control and power of choice creates this vacuum that causes your stomach to lurch up to your throat and the back of your tongue to clamp down.

However, when we push, cross or tear down our own boundaries, that's closer to Bare Naked Bravery. When the power of choice remains on our side and we still choose to break through or jump over boundaries, we exhibit courage.

Who determined the location of this boundary?

Sometimes we end up adopting boundaries unintentionally. I've been known to default to tradition or industry standards for my boundaries. As time progresses, asking myself this question "Who determined the location of this boundary?" helps to reveal that 1) yes, it is my boundary, 2) but I allowed someone else to build it there. Recognizing that truth sometimes alleviates a world of struggle.

The existence of this book is a great example. Musicians and professional songwriters aren't typically devoting their time and career to writing books and hosting a podcast. It's different. It's not normal. It's not the industry standard. I wrestled with that fact before, during, and soon after starting on this adventure. But as I recognized these boundaries belonging originally to the music industry, it freed me to be different and break industry standard. At one point I had allowed the industry standard to set in place a boundary for my career. Recognizing that wasn't *my* placement of the boundary and that it was still my boundary, immediately I felt how much easier it was to be "weird."

Context

"When the whole world is silent, even one voice becomes powerful."—Malala Yousafzai

What is weird and what isn't? It's really a discussion about environment and context, which is the second ingredient of bravery. It's an important one, too. One of my podcast listeners recently asked me, "How do we know how 'out' to be?"

Similar to our "Mmbop" example, if you're at a cosplay convention wearing an elaborately engineered outfit with robotic features, face paint, and a lot of spandex then "Woah. That's cool!" Your presence is honored there because the context is ideal! You're among people just like you who admire the 100-plus hours you've spent building this thing. You could probably run through the main convention floor screaming "My people! My people!" and you'd get cheers of agreement.

But if you wear that same outfit to your old high school buddy's wedding (without the bride's approval) then the context is likely not ideal. Running through the dance floor in the middle of the bride and groom's first dance screaming "My people! My people!" would get you gasps and a dirty look from the bride.

When your Bravery is starkly contrasted by your environment, it's either a really brave or stupidly insensitive thing to do.

Flashing your neighbors would be a similar example. Walking down the street totally nude would get you arrested. (Boundaries exist for a reason, remember?) But walking around your house totally nude might get you some bedroom action with your honey.

Context is related to Vulnerability because these walls, boundaries, and environments are a distinguishing factor in whether you're being brave or just being stupid or rude.

If I took my shirt off at a concert on stage, yikes, I probably just lost my mind. If I took my shirt off in front of total strangers, we'd better be in the context of a gym locker room. But if I took my shirt off in front of a sweetheart of a boyfriend after I had just told him about my experiences with self-image and an eating disorder, if I just told him how scared I was about being seen fully with the lights still on, and I *still* revealed myself? That's Bare Naked Bravery. Literally.

Our environment is such an important factor in how our vulnerability is received.

Feng Shui or Funk Shooey?

At the end of a cello lesson a couple years ago, I announced an apology for the state of my studio. Coffee mugs, sheet music, and old mail was strewn about every surface of the room. "I am so sorry for how disastrous everything looks! Please forgive the mess! I need to do a clean sweep and take care of some things!" The student's mother and I then had a good laugh about how it happens without even thinking about it. She then told me their family calls it "Funk Shooey" when the Feng Shui of a room is *not* ideal. I could just picture this mom walking into one of her child's room exclaiming "Oh! Yikes. Honey, the funk shooey in here is putrid! Let's clean things up a bit!"

The times in my life where I've attempted to do something brave and it doesn't get well-received, *usually* meant that I wasn't considering whether the context of my bravery was prepared to receive it. Like for instance, the time I poured my heart out into a song for a guy. He accepted the song and rejected me. Ouch. That hurt.

What made that an act of bravery to me, is that I already considered the context. It was unlikely that he would take me back after such a long time apart. I knew he would probably say "no." If I were to relive that moment, I might not have sent it to him.

I knew I was probably going to get rejected. But there was a tiny thread of possibility, which is why I went for it. Part of me was bracing for the rejection. I probably sang that song with a wince on my face, not from hitting high notes but from preparing for the inevitable pain.

Rejection

"I'm going to keep talking. I can get my voice out there. I walked in the woods. That was enough. I'm done with that and now I'm back."—Hillary Clinton on her post 2016 election resilience

Some folks wear rejection letters with pride. I've heard stories of seasoned writers hanging framed letters of rejection above their writing desks as proof of being a "real" writer. I've heard pickup artists and salesmen who consider every rejection as a milemarker on the way to a "yes." If you're just playing a numbers game, then yes, rejection is just a symbol of getting closer to what you want.

In some cases, knowing that 1) the rejection might suck but 2) we are resilient creatures—can make the feat of bravery more doable. More specifically asking the question: "What would happen if I *didn't* risk rejection?"

Here's how this process looked for me yesterday ...

- *What if I write the book and everyone hates it?* Well, it'll sting for awhile and I might need to put my production calendar on hold for a bit. But it wouldn't kill me.

- *What if I write the book and everyone loves it?* Hmm... I'd have to deal with the unknown of what my career would look like. I don't know those answers, even that is scary, possibly more scary than the book being rejected.

- *What would happen if I didn't write the book?*
First of all, the last three years of research and
conversations would feel wasted, like I didn't
give it all the chance they deserved. I'd also
have a lot of unresolved angst for not following
through with something I care so deeply about.
But I'd also never know if someone out there
really needed to hear what I have to say.

Writing this book, asking that guy on a date, hiring
my first assistant, going on my first solo West Coast
tour—these are all moments when I asked (or
should've asked) that question, acknowledging what
would happen if I didn't take the risk, and following
up with what might happen if I *did* take the risk?
Those are some gutsy questions to ask yourself. I
wholeheartedly recommend it.

So what do you do when you've "put yourself out
there" only to be rejected? Rejection is not a bowl of
daisies, especially if you're not used to it.

It's a pretty wise and perfectly acceptable idea to go
nurse your wounds. Go back to the safety of your
boundaries. Find the right environment to nurture
your bravery. Seek the comfort of being near your
people. Rediscover why you did that brave thing in
the first place.

Rejection is the absence of belonging. It's the
heightened feeling of being a "fish out of water."
Everything feels exposed and out of place all at once.
Being banished to the other side of the playground
is the same feeling as not getting a part in the play.

Knowing your physical body is "wrong" or in the wrong place or shaped the wrong way or even the wrong color is all ultimately the same sensation. How you react to that rejection depends on your own story of belonging and those reactions show up with varying degrees of severity.

Rejection preys on our fears of "not enough" or "too much" and will turn those fears into isolation and separateness. It's tempting never to trust anyone again, especially after the amount of online dating I've done. Laughably and unfortunately, I'm not the only one with that kind of boundary in their love life for those reasons, but I digress.

Metaphorically retracting your hand from the stove after getting burned is an appropriate reaction to pain. Similarly, isolation after rejection is the easy answer, most of the time it too is the appropriate answer.

However, there will be times after rejection when returning to your place of belonging with an open heart, even with a wound of rejection, is the hardest kind of bravery you'll ever step into. In those moments of post-rejection, it takes true vulnerability to remain open and connected—to not shut off from the world completely—to not overcompensate for the pain by building extravagant walls. After rejection, we continue to practice feats of bravery by reconnecting to belonging with the same thin skin we were born with.

Where is your place of belonging?

I don't know about you, but my sense of belonging was extremely warped. Many of us turn to discipline, rules, and regulations for salvation from rejection. I've tried to find belonging from soooo many places, and failed.

My culture and family of origin told me I was too much. So I gathered those externally motivated boundaries tightly around, cinched in the waist, cut the calories, and went to sleep fantasizing about taking knives to my belly fat and thighs. I came of age eating fistfuls of rejection for breakfast, lunch, and dinner.

A spiritual family provided boundaries for living a life of abundance and freedom from pain. They promised a sense of belonging with strings attached to being ultimately sinful and destined to hell. When I came to them with a "confession of sin" via an out-of-control eating disorder, I was met with a message from the elders and my spiritual mentors. They told me freedom from this personal hell and sense of rejection would require a few steps. First I needed to forgive my parents, no questions asked. Second, we'd need to pray it all away. Then if that didn't work, whipping my mind into shape through memorizing ancient text would do the trick.

Like thousands of Americans before me, when family and a spiritual life didn't provide a sense of belonging, I turned to the military. I'm not the only person who has found solace in the romantic tradition of fighting for and fostering this feeling of belonging, albeit nationalistic belonging. In an almost-valiant effort to ward off the eating disorder (as if it were a big nasty monster that existed outside myself) I discovered the strength to swear off laxatives and binge dieting during my freshman year of college through placing the control of my sense of belonging into the hands of the United States Air Force, ROTC.

I raised my right hand, said the sacred vow, and in an instant the clear lines, undeniable rules, and standard uniform that fit me like a glove provided a safety net and permission to simply be all I could be.

I adored their rules which gave me space from my own life-threatening rejection. That didn't change the fact that I still didn't belong.

I loved the traditions of a military lifestyle but was too musical, too artsy, and too eager to think outside the box. I was too stubborn to submit my morality and mortality to some guy farther up the ranks. I was too feminine to not get called out for special treatment. I was too sensitive and even that was getting "worn down" by the persistent come-ons, gender exclusion, and off-colored humor.

Leaving the military didn't fix it. Outside the manufactured walls of nationalistic belonging was an all-consuming tidal wave of rejection. I lasted six months outside those walls of national standards of excellence and found myself walking up a dorm stairwell, crumbling to the ground, sinking under the weight of a small box of laxatives.

Some would say this is a Grimm's fairy tale version of the classic children's book "Are You My Mother?" Except instead of running around to various parts of the animal kingdom posing the same question over and over, I was endlessly running around to every nook and cranny of life to ask "Do I belong here?"

Nope. Nope. Nope. Rejection. Rejection. Reject.

This lack of belonging affected my ability to stay vulnerable. It still does. (That is part of my personal bravery.) Yet I have seen first-hand that encountering life with bravery one day at a time unveils this truth: belonging is impossible to find outside yourself.

It's a tall order to be unshakably understood, cared for, heard, and accepted by an organization, significant other, hobby or career. Unshakable belonging for just simply being? Just existing? Just as you are, without doing anything to deserve it? Outside the realm of religious orders, national pride and cultural expectations?

Seeking your belonging within boundaries that aren't yours to begin with will eventually lead to places that exclude you from "them" or "it" whatever or whomever they may be. External sources of belonging will always find reasons to exclude you.

Honesty

Belonging, true belonging, is not found externally. I stopped the exercising and the rule making. I stopped the fits of merciless rage-running around manmade lakes. I stopped distracting myself from rejection with false sensations of "home."

I began to learn my own boundaries and to find my innate sense of belonging. That alone is a feat of internal bravery and not a solo adventure for everyone. I started being honest with myself, especially during the moments of feeling like a misfit or a reject. It's not always a safe thing to do alone, at least it wasn't for me. I needed to call for help.

I had to get still. I had to stop the noise and listen. I had to open up. I had to be honest with myself, be honest within myself. It was dirty, messy, and what I found most assuredly spilled outside the lines of acceptable public behavior. A lot of anger, tears, and pent up expression anxiously awaited even the faint glimmer of release.

Being honest about your shitty situation or your throat-clenching fears is the perfect place to find your bravery. Entertaining somewhat abrasive, unanswered questions and unknown answers is the birthplace for bravery.

For example, it takes substantial guts to honestly admit that you'd rather live someone else's life (in a book, movie, or tv show) than to live your own life with your precious kids and spouse by your side. This admission alone is bravery, especially after you've reached the end of the 13th season of that one TV show during your only vacation time for the year.

When you toss your leggings in the trash of the university bathroom and go commando in a mini skirt, not because it's sexy, but because your laxative abuse caused you to literally shit your pants on the way to class? When that terrifyingly hilarious race against your failing intestines led to a tearful, yet silent admission in the bathroom stall. That is brave honesty.

When you're packing your whole life into storage boxes and you truly don't know when you'll see your favorite plates and mugs again, when you can honestly acknowledge the fear of the unknown and still manage to pack up your favorite stack of books, that is Bare Naked Bravery—especially when it doesn't feel courageous. Like bravery, honesty can be really uncomfortable.

Becoming fluent in bravery requires vulnerable honesty, even if it's under our breath or just to ourselves. Even when you're the only audience member of this honesty, what comes after it can be so, so good.

I'll be the first to admit that radical honesty is not always smart. It certainly isn't productive to lean on honesty as your only policy. Saying things like "Well honey, it's just the truth" is how people lose friends and family. Radical honesty by itself is just called being an asshole. But when radical honesty is also sensitive to the context and risk, there's a certain kindness found in that kind of bravery, isn't there?

When we combine these three ingredients together —our context, measure of risk, and honesty— vulnerability is close at hand and usually bravery soon follows. Here are some all too familiar honest statements, which, depending on the environment (context), audience (context), and measure of risk/ safety herald massive statements of vulnerability...

"Well, this is certainly a new low."
"I'm about to have a panic attack. I can't breathe."
"Everything just feels so out of control and I hate it."
"Something is really not right in our relationship."
"He is driving me absolutely crazy."
"I need to move out."
"She hurt you and that hurts me."
"I never wanted this to happen."
"I think I've got a crush on him."
"I've always wanted to do that."
"I love you."

The words uttered *after* those exposed statements of honesty are the difference between jaded bitterness and Bare Naked Bravery. Follow up any of the above statements of radical honesty with one of the following statements and the story immediately gets an opportunity for resolution and fresh air.

"Would you be willing to help me?"
"Woah, I need to take a minute."

"Do *you* know what's wrong here?"
"How did we get here?"
"What should I do now?"

These statements, questions, and exposed displays of honesty make room for the inevitable vulnerable strength that follows. Simply put, here's how these 3 ingredients can contribute to our vulnerability and subsequent bravery...

Honesty: You've locked yourself out of the house.
Context: It's cold outside and you have no phone.
Risk: Frost bite.
Vulnerability: Ask the new neighbors for a phone to call to the locksmith.

Honesty: A new rock-bottom.
Context: You've been here before.
Risk: Losing more than you already have.
Vulnerability: Calling your AA sponsor, therapist, or a friend.

Honesty: Things aren't working in the relationship
Context: You've been together for five years.
Risk: A relationship on perpetual life-support.
Vulnerability: "Maybe it's time to take a break?"

Honesty: Too much stimulus is not healthy tonight.
Context: You said you'd go to a party with your friends.
Risk: Looking like a "loser" and letting people down.
Vulnerability: Changing your RSVP status.

Vulnerability might be what happens when you're absolutely butchering the song, the shift, the words, the chords, the speech, the book, the presentation— and you keep going anyways... or maybe it looks like stopping, taking a deep breath, and starting again.

But if bravery were just vulnerability, we'd be running around with emotional bruises and measuring walls. The thing which gives a breath to the risk of vulnerability, is a hope for something more than merely exposure. In the next chapter you'll see how imagination, made from defiant expectation, constraints, and a vision of possibility, can create hope for something more than just rules, exposure, boundaries, and regulations of risk.

Imagination = Defiant Expectation + Vision of Possibility + Constraints

The word "imagination" might sound clean, fluffy and harmless to some, but cleanliness, logic, and innocence are far from how I'd describe imagination. Imagination is a force of nature, a force to be reckoned with. It is messy. It doesn't make sense or draw straight lines, and it loves to be ridiculously fantastical.

Imagination can feel aloof and abstract without some anchors thrown down. The kind of imagination used to build bravery is made of rebellion, possibility, and limitations. While discussing bravery with as many people as would let me, these three recurring themes came up: 1) a stubbornness 2) because of a dream for something else 3) despite limitations.

If we go back to the classic brave feat of "jumping into a burning building" we can find all three of the elements of imagination. This feat of vulnerable strength requires a defiant expectation and vision that whoever is trapped inside the constraint of a building on fire will live after all is said and done.

Unadulterated, uncensored imagination is made of defiant expectation.

Defiant Expectation

"Even if I knew that tomorrow the world would go to pieces,
I would still plant my apple tree."—Martin Luther

To the chagrin of many adults older than I, the phrase "spiritual renewal of the mind" is tattooed to the back of my neck. I got it in college about a year after the dorm stairwell/box of laxatives night. What many people don't know is that this tattoo is aimed at my eating disorder. The season of life during which I got the tattoo was filled with fantastically defiant expectation. To this day, the writing on the back of my neck says, "You [eating disorder and anything else that threatens my life] will fuck with me no more."

When a former bandmate discovered I had a neck tattoo (my hair usually covers it), he made some joke about how the majority of neck tattoos are typically found on individuals who've spent time behind bars. In the moment we chuckled about it before going back to rehearsal.

But I've got news: mental illness, depression, OCD, and a slew of other symptoms sure did *feel* like an entrapment of steel bars. So maybe my choice of a hideable yet meaningful tattoo location was appropriate.

Writing something defiant on my body did not fix things on its own. But that's what made this tattoo so fantastic. And I don't mean fantastic in a "That's so great" kind of way. I mean fantastic in a fantastically imaginative kind of way. Only someone with a fantasy of living without the torment of a mental illness would do something as crazy as writing something about it permanently on their flesh.

I'm not a psychologist. I'm not a doctor. Far from it, I'm a musician with a degree in business. So I cannot say with any amount of medical or therapeutic professional confidence that things like eating disorders, alcoholism, drug addictions, codependency, and enabling are curable. Mental and emotional ghosts of all kinds "buzz the tower" of the haunted for a lifetime. Believe me, getting your tower buzzed by the ghosts of past struggles is definitely not as invigorating as watching Top Gun.

Even though I'd like to think I've been cured from a warped way of living/eating/breathing/thinking, I'm not going to pretend I don't have limitations, nor pretend that life is impermeable to external factors.

However, I have seen that those of us who entertain our imagination and can picture what a different life could be are the ones who can match our external lives most closely to the status of 'cured,' despite the staggering odds against us.

I had tea the other day with someone 30 years older than me, from a very different frame of mind and beliefs than my own. For the purposes of this book, let's call her Mary. She's a longtime friend of the family, whom I hadn't spoken to in years. She was curious about my story. This meant conversation inevitably rolled into my (long past) eating disorder experience and healing. Not surprisingly, this facet of my story brought up another subject—the biggest, hairiest subject for me to discuss, especially with someone who knows my family ... female attractiveness.

"A woman's appearance exists to please and attract a man," Mary said matter of factly after sipping her tea.

As a young girl, that message was the largest and most poisonous message I ever received, it came from all around me: family members, spiritual leaders, culture, media, peers ...

<gag>

But after all the years I've spent bravely battling my biggest fears I've learned a few tricks, mainly how valuable defiant expectation is.

So over a cup of tea in the middle of a little coffee shop overlooking the Chattahoochee River, this woman and I—who were brought up in a completely different worlds—discovered and discussed our disagreement over what men thought about "the attractiveness" of females. Because she's a friend of our family's I did my very *very* best to keep my cool and not totally lose my ever-loving feminist mind all over her...

As we talked it was clear that she has such a strong attachment to this myth that men are only attracted to skinny/fit women.

She said, "But Emily Ann, men act on what they see. They are visually wired. If what they see is not attractive, they won't act."

I was SHOCKED she would say this to my face, because I make absolutely no attempts to hide the fact that I do not fit into that category of culturally approved beauty standards. Today, I am very much curvy, plus size, and unabashedly fluffy. By saying what she did, she was also announcing "I believe no man will be attracted to you, Emily Ann."

My immediate and very audible response was "If that's true, then I guess it means I'll be single for the rest of my life."

You should've seen the look on her face, because even the notion of choosing to remain single for eternity is a "fish upstream" sentiment in the Southern States of the US. Why would anyone want to do anything different than getting married? Isn't that just how life is lived?

Taking a slow and (very) deep breath, I gathered everything I knew about my worldview, beliefs, and hopes for the world and quietly dove into my explanation, "Mary, I'm willing to forgo "normal life" in defiant expectation that 1) men aren't as shallow as their evolutionary and cultural standards and 2) that beauty is defined by so much more than those shallow standards. I believe this so much that I'm willing to defiantly live my life expecting more from my fellow humans and opposite sex. If that means I'll be single for the rest of my life, then so be it. But I refuse to succumb to partnering myself for life with someone who believes otherwise."

The combination of these subjects—beauty, personal appearance, and defiant expectation—is my wheelhouse and you don't mess with something I have a "Life PHD" in. I continued by telling her that if we went about life, politics, and business merely succumbing to the standards set by the world around us, we would see no progress, no change, no growth. We'd be victims of our lives. We'd be powerless.

I could tell by the somewhat bewildered and quizzical look on her face as we walked out of the coffeeshop that our afternoon conversation blew her mind wide open. It blew mine wide open too. In years previous, a conversation like that would've smashed me to bits and reduced me to tears.

Without defiant expectation, we have stagnancy. That or a pent-up amount of potential trapped behind walls blocking us from truly living. Without defiant expectation, we wouldn't have the Civil Rights Movement, American Revolution, Apple Computers, and poetry. Without defiant expectation in music we wouldn't have the massive wall of sound found in Mahler's Symphonies. We wouldn't have Lady Gaga's "Born This Way." We wouldn't have the breathtaking minimalism of Arvo Pärt's musical works.

Every time you see someone doing anything brave, somewhere in there you'll find their defiant expectation. That defiant expectation is founded upon a clarity that only a vision of possibility can bring.

Vision of Possibility

"Whisper you dream to a cloud
Ask the cloud to remember it."—Yoko Ono

To measure imagination is to measure your vision of possibility. I most admire the people in history who have said, "I will not stand for this." They entertained the possibility of someday, somehow living a different life. Not only did they conjure a different reality, they acted on it externally. It takes a true rebel to entertain expectations without validation from the outside world. Outward defiance, the kind that makes the history books, starts within the internal landscape of a rebel.

In her autobiography, Rosa Parks corrected the rumors of her motivation behind refusing to move seats in the segregated Alabama bus, "People always say that I didn't give up my seat because I was tired, but that isn't true. I was not tired physically, or no more tired than I usually was at the end of a working day. I was not old, although some people have an image of me as being old then. I was forty-two. No, the only tired I was, was tired of giving in."

It may be true that historic statements of defiance came with the context of being just too tired to give a rat's ass about living in a former way of being. But to permit yourself to get to that point of exhausting reason and 'decency' is to also entertain your imagination. Reaching limitations of endurance is what brings forth this clarity of possibility. It is from these places of constraint that we can envision our options and potential beyond those constraints. This is because internal and external constraints can reveal the raw potential of your imagination.

She was right. A look at Rosa Parks' mug shot on that day will confirm she was far from physically exhausted. Behind her eyes you see a fire dancing on the line of indecent reason.

We don't know precisely when Rosa Parks' imagination birthed the notion that we could live in a world where a bus seat can give rest to someone regardless of their skin's color. But we do know that living in a culture that did not validate Rosa Parks' imagination created a friction within her, a friction so powerful that it broke societal norms. The constraints of American culture pulled against the boundaries of her personhood and her vision of a world free of racism. So there she sat with vulnerable strength and defiant expectation. Founded upon a fantastic imagination, her actions sparked a changemaking fire in our nation.

Imagination rarely bothers with asking reality for permission or a second opinion.

On that day in 1955, Rosa Parks' imagination broke through her intuition to give permission to become vulnerably, honestly, ultimately, historically, defiantly stubborn. She did not move from her seat. She did not give in.

As J.K. Rowling said at her 2008 Harvard Commencement speech, "We do not need magic to change the world, we carry all the power we need inside ourselves already: we have the power to imagine better." At which point all the publishers of motivational quote calendars furiously jotted down their vision of next season's cover image.

But imagination can go both ways—dark and light, hope and despair, big and small. Our imaginations can hop on the small, dark, morbid train as quick as a duck on a Junebug.

In the same speech, Rowling continued, "Choosing to live in narrow spaces leads to a form of mental agoraphobia, and that brings its own terrors. I think the willfully unimaginative see more monsters. They are often more afraid." That soundbite didn't make the cut for motivational calendar quotes, but it remains equally true.

Reading Shadows

As children, a lot of us shared a fear of darkness. I don't know about you, but I hated it when the babysitter would close the door even an inch too far. The trees outside combined with the city lights would make terrifying shapes on my bedroom walls. Depending on the wind and activity of the shadows displayed in the glow of the street, I was known to summon all my strength to run out of my bedroom in my footie pajamas squealing with terror.

One Christmas morning at around 2am, after the "elves" had gone to sleep, something woke me from my childhood slumber. I snuck out of the bedroom to crawl in bed with my parents. But on my way down the hall, I caught a glimpse of this ENORMOUS dark square-ish figure with glowing eyes of different colors. Thank God I was potty-trained, because I would've peed my pajamas right then and there. Later that morning, rather than run out into the living room to begin opening presents like the American kid I was in the early 90's, I stayed in mom and dad's bedroom. When they eventually woke up I told them there was a big dark monster in the living room with glowing eyes. It turns out "Santa" had brought a hand-built dollhouse, complete with tiny electric chandeliers and miniature stained glass lamps in every window.

We've all been reading shadows since we were little. We see the unknown variables of our lives unfold and then we leave whatever's available—our knowledge, reason, and past experiences—to fill in the blanks. I don't know a single person who hasn't worked themselves into a tizzy of terror by thinking a little too hard about what a shadow or unknown means, figuratively or literally. It takes imagination to read shadows.

Nervous girlfriends who've had their hearts broken before will go from "Hmm ... he hasn't texted me today." to "What?! He hasn't texted me today?! I must not be _____ enough." Anxiety-ridden business owners go from celebrating a success over Friday's networking happy hour to the pits of financial recession at dinner later that night.

And who's got two thumbs and threatening moments of existential crises when she checks her inbox and hasn't received a new email? This girl.

We all read shadows. If we look close enough, reading into the shadows, voids, and vacuums of our lives can ultimately reveal more about our own prejudices or hopes than that which is actually creating the shadow to begin with. We do this all the time with our stories and with the stories of others. Our shadow reading reveals ourselves and our imaginations. Interpretations of shadows reveal more about the interpreter's imagination than the object creating the shadow.

Our heart and mind recognizes somewhat familiar blanks and fills them with our subconscious. Fear sees darkness smeared across the walls and swoops in with total and complete doom through utter fantasy. When it comes to constraints and shadows, our imagination takes the darkness, unknowns, and voids and fills in the blanks with whatever is available.

Our intuition catches wind of this chaos and demands we take action of some kind, even if that action is to become frozen solid in fear. But only in dark rooms does the smallest light make the largest shadows. It's true. How we choose to entertain our possibilities can alter our realities. Through our imagination, we create the internal world from which we live on the outside.

However, eventually imagination will meet constraints. But constraints can be a good thing to mix with Imagination. Imagination, when mixed with vulnerable honesty, clarifies our possible and perhaps probable realities.

Constraints

Great artists do not make art without fear, but despite fear.—Julia Cameron

The beauty behind exhaustion and extreme circumstances is that they reveal the raw, untamed power of our imagination, the same imagination that existed within us all along. Sometimes finding ourselves at the end of our rope is the only way to reveal the untapped imagination that later becomes Bravery.

Knowing the speed limit allows us to imagine at what point we could possibly get pulled over for being late to that one thing we were supposed to be at 15 minutes ago. Knowing the amount of time remaining in someone's battle with cancer allows us to imagine what a really good goodbye will look like. Knowing your wife's limitations on socks being left in the crease of the couch might help you imagine either a divorce or a blissful sex life.

When we combine the honestly vulnerable realities of our circumstances with our internal imaginations, we permit ourselves the freedom of choice held within those constraints. We can begin to dream and improvise toward what life could become.

Everything has constraints. I repeat, EVERYTHING has constraints. There are only so many hours in a day. The budget has a limit. The credit card has a maximum. The laws of physics can only be stretched so far. Gravity will always pull. Humans will eventually reach their expiration date and so will that jug of milk in your refrigerator.

Some constraints might stay the same. Most will change. Life will always unfold new constraints for us. I can guarantee something will always change. There will always be parts of life that involve some variable we cannot control. Someone's going to say something at the wrong time. Some detail will be forgotten. Some car won't see the red light. Some beret-wearing poetry professor is going to give you an F, not because your poem was terrible, but because he's bitter about life.

If you're part of the 'abundant mindset' Koolaid drinkers, like I am, then the notion that it's possible to thrive within scarcity probably has you reaching for your burning sage to clear such blasphemous words from the room.

Newsflash: It is possible to thrive abundantly within and alongside scarcity. This is the way of defiant expectation, vision of possibility, imagination and ultimately Bare Naked Bravery.

Though constraints sound stifling and restricting, they aren't. Constraints are a very good thing, especially when it comes to creativity and the courage that comes from it.

Constraints aren't all "bad."

Without the constraints of plumbing, we would just have a bunch of sewage puddles at the bottom of the basement. Without the constraint of the window blocking the wind, we'd have really cold drafts in January and hot air blowing through in July. Without the constraint on the bowling alley provided by a bumper, your niece would have a bajillion gutter balls. Without the constraints within the component of steel, we'd have really flimsy cars and houses. Without the constraint of geography, there would be no valleys, beaches, mountains.

Another good example of this is the cello bow. It's a stick with some horse hair shoved into both ends. It does not create sound on its own. The bow's sole job is to create friction against the constraint of the string, just enough to sustain the string's aggravation, also known as its vibration. If the bow did not exist, I can guarantee there wouldn't be many folks running up after performances to tell me how much they "just love the sound of the cello." It's true. Without the constraints provided by the string and the bow, we'd just have a bunch of pluckin' cellists.

Another example of constraints: Any time I return to the US from a cultural adventure, grocery shopping is one of the first things that needs to be done. This is laughably one of the most endearing yet disturbing settings for reverse culture shock. It is in the grocery store that I am reminded how difficult it is to choose a box of cereal in the US. There is an entire double-sided aisle reserved for starchy, sugary breakfast food intended to be held by a bowl. An entire aisle. Don't even get me started on toothpaste.

Having sensitive teeth certainly allows us to imagine leaving the toothpaste aisle in under 60 seconds. Thank God. Knowing your requirements for a non-sugary cereal allows you to imagine leaving the cereal aisle in under 30 seconds. The options in those grocery aisles are limited for those sensitive toothed, sugar-free folks.

In the business world, cereal and toothpaste happen to be two of the hardest markets for a new product or brand to penetrate. This is because of the sheer number of options consumers already possess. Too many options prevent consumers from exploring new products.

My personal habits as a consumer of these items fall right in line with this theory. Option overwhelm all the way! Regardless of the state of my culture shock, my go-to tactic for conquering both of those aisles in the grocery store is to 1) throw my hands up in the air, 2) make some exclamation about how weird our country is, 3) find the product I've always picked, and then 4) get the hell out of the aisle.

However, if I go down the toothpaste aisle with any constraint, let's say having sensitive teeth, that automatically reduces my product options from a bajillion to about eight. With the constraint of having sensitive teeth, it's much easier to make a toothpaste selection.

Here's another example: Several choreographer friends of mine participate in one of my favorite annual modern dance performances. At this event, the choreographers have a time constraint of 3 to 5 minutes and a spatial constraint of a 4-by-4-foot stage. You should see the genius that comes from these constraints!

The time and spatial restrictions on these brilliant choreographers have the effect of permitting more attention on the other elements of the performance: the spatial height of the choreography, the dancers' costuming, the music, the focus and execution of body movements. The time and spatial constraints give enough permission for the overall performance to refine, focus, and blossom.

When we rely on and acknowledge our constraints we can focus our attention on what really matters. Our constraints help us identify our other priorities.

So yes, constraints can be a very good thing ... if we use them.

I'd be a billionaire if I had a penny for every time I've said or heard a version of "Maybe if I _[insert constraint here]_ then I will be able to _[insert new outcome for life]_!" Some of us, including myself, have an impulse to clamp down and self-impose constraints to manipulate the outcome of something.

It's tempting to think, maybe if we work harder, make more (or fewer) rules, more (or fewer) boundaries, set a stricter diet, tighten the purse strings, practice harder/longer, get up a little earlier, then things will finally go our way. It's tempting to think that doing all these things will prevent that-which-I-don't-want-to-change, from its inevitable and unavoidable change. Ha!

Imagine a yard hose. It's spread across the lawn because a certain someone didn't wrap it back up correctly. The spigot hasn't been turned off tightly enough, so the shower nozzle at the other end is threatening to bust loose. If you leave the spigot on long enough, the water pressure will find its way through a weak spot. It'll begin to escape in a trickle or a tiny little spurt. The teeny rainbows from the pinholes in the hose are cute, but the ongoing release of pressure in these unintended areas of the hose will make a bigger hole. Those cute, little, tiny rainbows will die and turn to puddles. Eventually, there will be water everywhere and the yard will get muddy and messy much faster than you think.

In a similar way, clamping down on self-imposed internal constraints by avoiding/fighting/ignoring life's external constraints means the pressure of potential and that-which-could-be will keep building if we do not give it an outlet. There will simultaneously be too much and not enough. This stress on either side of these constraints will leave us damaging our adrenal system to the point of total fatigue and failure. Something will have to give way.

Where am I going with this? Rather than clamp down and pile on self-imposed constraints or rather than run from/ignore our constraints...

Here's what I suggest: Use Constraints Like a Tool

Our constraints are only useful if we allow ourselves to see them that way. So rather than seeing constraints (be they time, spatial, financial, emotional, etc.) as something to run away from, fight against, mask with our "abundant mindsets," or blatantly ignore, we can instead learn to practice our lives differently by seeing the constraints as a *tool* for a creative outlet.

So how do we stop fighting against or running away from our constraints and begin to use them as a tool?

Congratulations, you're reading the right book. ;) Also, good question.

As you might've already gathered, creativity thrives on constraints. Creativity is always seeking out the next new fangled point of expansion, so perhaps we could, at the very core of things, describe creativity as potential bound by constraints. There's always a craving for freedom within creativity.

So if we are to bravely make new things, new dances, new solutions, new products, new strides with our fear, new friendships, new anything—there must be a measure of sensing our limits, our boundaries and our constraints. Creativity is naturally driven by the desire for freedom or release from those constraints. Since creativity is one half of the growing cycle of creative courage, it too is driven by the desire for freedom and release. The same old thing is just never enough.

Here's an example: If you sit still for a very long time, you'll probably discover your leg is cramping or losing blood flow or your face starts to itch. This is because somewhere inside you, there is a constraint impinging on your body's freedom. Somewhere inside your body there is anticipation for something, quite possibly relief from your current slouchy posture.

If you follow that desire and follow the craving for freedom from constraint by being sensitive to the constraint and not necessarily avoiding it, you might begin to adjust your body's position—perhaps by lying, standing, or sitting straighter.

By becoming educated and skilled in knowing, using, and improvising within your constraints, you'll begin to anticipate the available paths to your desires, plan for your responses, and get to a place of relief with much less fighting and flighting.

FYI: Fear is a Constraint.

When your fear is not acknowledged, its symptoms have a tendency to leak out in places we'd rather not have them leak out. The fear of danger unexpectedly spews onto your kids when you're on a road trip. The fear of change emotionally leaks out with tiny passive aggressions towards your co-workers. The fear of failure soaks the boardroom tables with unintentional timidity in your client meetings. Fear can even freeze into depression and addictive behavior cycles.

Fear shows up like an iceberg, with an overall mass seven to 10 times larger than what we can see from the surface. Anxiety. Tension. Deafening silences. They point to what lies under the surface of these constraints. Unbeknownst to even the best of us, we tend to lash out at the symptoms, instead of the real issues. Fears of (un)worthiness lie under financial and relational stresses. The desire to be heard lies within explosive group dynamics. There is always something more just under the surface.

Fear smacks down its opposition faster than Hulk Hogan did in the 1990s and it can show up as self-sabotage in almost every area of life. It's because of fear that we'll trash the seeds of some pretty great ideas.

Yes, generally fear is all dark and gloomy and scary. Yes, some of your fears might sound like they come from Eeyore's hometown. But there is a lighter side to fear.

As with constraints, your fear does not have to be a bad thing. In fact, it can be a very, very good thing.

Though our fears have the potential to clamp down on life, there are some really beautiful gifts held within each of them.

For example, If we weren't afraid of burning ourselves on the stove, some of us would probably need to wear oven mitts at all hours of the day. If we weren't afraid of rejection, we'd find ourselves in relationships that weren't worth the effort. If it weren't for a fear of germs/viruses, the world would be a dirty health hazard! It if weren't for the fear of worthiness, some of us might not value effort. Same goes for the fear of failing or fear of scarcity.

Thankfully, fear can become a comrade. Over time we can learn to laugh with our fear and consider it a friend. Go ahead, roll your eyes. But there's a need to make time to listen to and get to know our fears in between life's battles.

Fear and other constraints are not the enemy. They are sheep in wolf's clothing.

Here's how: If we really knew our fears and constraints or at least felt somewhat comfortable knowing they exist, wouldn't our future battles seem less daunting?

Listening to and understanding the fear is the key to using it.

If we learn to listen to our fear of scarcity, we can understand it might actually be a love of safety and dependability. Maybe if we listen to our fear of success, we can uncover the reality that we don't actually want the promotion, maybe we just want the extra vacation days that come with it. Perhaps your fear of being-out-of-control was fostered by a parent or spouse who had their own out-of-control fear of failure or being unloved. Maybe it's not a fear of dying, but a drive to keep living a better life. Perhaps your fear of having true talent is actually a disguised fear of being seen.

If we can practice and become skilled at listening to our fears and acknowledging our other constraints, there can be hope at the bottom of our rock bottom. There can even be hope when we surprisingly bump up against a new constraint. It's not the end of the world. Even more so when we allow vulnerability, imagination and improvisation to guide our listening to the fear, we might uncover fear's gift to us: creative courage and the Bare Naked Bravery to act on it.

By using our defiant expectation and vision of possibility with acknowledging constraints we are given the opportunity to listen to our creative impulses and find the courage to make something more of life. But our recipe for Bare Naked Bravery is still incomplete without a sense of action and power to make things happen. In the next chapter, we'll unfold what it means to skillfully move in the midst of your environment, limitations, and objectives.

Improvisation = Intuition + Friction + Power of Choice

"Don't be intimidated by what you don't know. That can be your greatest strength and ensure that you do things differently from everyone else."—Sara Blakely

Because of my Southern upbringing, lightning bolts are not the sign of impending doom that most North Westerners see. Instead the flashes of light across the summer skies are merely signs of the changing weather. Any threats of lightning told told the kids it was time to get out of the pool and told the parents to take their last swigs of Lone Star beer. A lot of neighborhood barbecue parties ended with the sight of lightning in the sky. We all knew lightning and swimming do not mix.

I'll never forget swimming late on a moonless night with the Texas sky turning a rich navy. I could feel the water cooling from the earlier triple-digit weather while the evening "cold front" would blow in from about 200 miles away. It makes for an entertaining evening to mix the hot and cold like that in the sky. The sight of that distant bolt of lightning racing across the sky was thrilling.

Those flashes reminded us how thin was our notion of "safety." With nothing but the Spandex of a swimsuit for protection, we would witness Earth's sheer power rip across the sky. Only a blink away from assured death, we reluctantly welcomed the warning to get out of danger and get out of the water. Fear mixed with exhilaration.

Lightning bolts might arrive accompanied by the kind of thunder that would rattle any foundation, but these bolts also brought a flash of clarity from the heavens. In an instant the landscape would flash awake. Pathways would become irrefutably clear, especially on moonless stormy summer nights.

In life, the lightning isn't always so obvious. Sometimes the warnings and red flags are so distant you have to ask around, "Was that lightning? Am I crazy? Should I get out of here?"

However distant the lightning is, I urge you to lean into the clarity these bolts of light offer you. Heed their warnings. Towel off the water. Find your safe places. And sit back. Watch what unfolds. You might get to see the sky show off in a beautiful way.

In this chapter we talk about the action element of bravery. Vulnerability and imagination are good together, but when we can improvise using our vulnerability and imagination, that's when the real bravery occurs.

Remember that these three main ingredients of bravery are like a three-part venn diagram. It's possible to have improvisation and imagination, but without the vulnerability usually we make choices that don't involve our measure of safety or surroundings (a recipe for regret).

Listening for the subtle messages from the summer night sky or something else and then choosing to act accordingly, that is the essence of improvisation. In this chapter we'll unfold a bit of the mystery wrapped into my favorite skills of bravery: listening to your intuition, sensing friction, and using your power of choice.

Intuition

> *"Inspiration enters through the window of irrelevance."*— M.C. Richards

There will be times when your constraints don't seem to allow for much improvisation. Despite those limitations and contextual expectations, your intuition is worth listening to, even in the midst of irrefutable surroundings and circumstances. Our intuition is the "safety valve" for moments of bravery because it's not always appropriate to close our eyes, white knuckle it, and barrel through a given moment. Driving a car is a stellar example. Please. Keep your eyes open and hands on the steering wheel on the road while driving. But if you begin to feel metaphorical bumps and rattles, heed those warnings!

Our intuition might have an inkling of something that our intellect cannot explain right away. This happens because our subconscious processes information infinitely faster than our intellect can, so when intuition sends us the feeling that something isn't right or that we should lean in a specific direction, often it's spot on.

We override our intuitive instincts by blatantly ignoring or explaining them away out of a duty to civility or not wanting to be rude by potentially hurting someone's feelings. Sometimes our intuition asks us to do or say (or not do or not say) something that not everyone would approve of. But nine times out of 10 I wish I had listened to the quiet, unexplainable impulses of my intuition over the louder, belligerent constraints and explainable logic I found myself in:

- "Surely this random craigslist person who can move in on Monday will be a fine roommate."
- "This guy might be a bit abrasive with that poor waitress, but I'm sure he'll warm up after a couple more dates."
- "Something feels a little strange about this place, but everyone else is so freakin' excited I don't think I care!"
- "Susie worked so hard at this dinner and I am soo hungry, but this salad feels a little slimy..."

Alternatively, the times I did listen to my intuition resulted in the best decisions I've ever made.

- In fifth grade when selecting instruments, "The cello? Sure!"

- In college, switching majors for the fourth time, "I don't know why everyone's fussing about these business classes, they're pretty easy to me ... Maybe I should take a few more of them."
- The night before everyone else got food poisoning, "Nah, for some reason I don't want another bite of that chicken."

When I know I'm going head-first into a situation where I won't have a lot of flexibility, I've found that consciously leaving room for my intuition to have a say makes being in the midst of those stressful constraints a little easier. In this way not everything feels like "do or die."

For instance, when I'm giving a talk or teaching, I know it's more important to have my general objective and talking points ready. This extra space allows for more opportunity to incorporate my intuition and ability to "read the room" for what my audience *needs* me to say. This ultimately works better for everyone than watching me read a rigid script.

Intuition overlaps with vulnerability because listening to the quiet nudges of both require the same practice in sensitivity. Learning to build this strong sensitivity circles back to the failure required to become a fluent improvisationalist. We are born with intuitive instinct, but we learn to listen to it through falling and stumbling through extensive practice and attentive observation.

The spirality and mutual leaning-on that creativity and courage have in common is shaped by the circuitousness of intuition and vulnerability. Wow, that's a mouthful. What I mean is this: Intuition is the action and movement ingredient of bravery while vulnerability is its exposure. Both require sensitivity by listening to the risks (vulnerability) and listening to the nudges (intuition).

Let's dive a little further into this clarity of intuition. I've seen there are two types of guidance available to use as it pertains to bravery: internal guidance and external guidance.

Internal Guidance

Types of internal guidance from your intuition might show up in the forms of a sudden clamping down of your throat during a group conference call or that weird goosebump feeling you get while listening to someone say something mindblowing. Goosebumps also happen when that creepy unexplainable cold feeling crawls across your feet at a movie theater even though there's not a tangible draft.

Your internal guidance system might tell you to stay strong, be stubborn, and stand firm.

As a collaborative musician, I've learned to hone the internal guidance of my intuition through failed attempts at "holding down the tempo" for the rest of the orchestra. By ignoring my internal guidance system and getting easily swayed to rushing the beats (usually because violinists love to go too fast. *wink*) the rest of the piece suffers, especially when it's time for the basses to have the melody and the tempo is now too fast to fathom.

Sometimes your internal guidance will prompt you to move and be flexible. Let's say one holiday weekend, the lady behind the airline desk tells you your flight just got canceled and you suddenly have a way of relaxation rather than bout of culturally induced anxiety. Those are the moments to listen up and lean into that "abnormal" reaction. By staying in that calm state of mind, you might have the eyes to see two folks with a bumper sticker of your destination, strike up a chat, and split a taxi. Default anxiety would've made you blind to these creative opportunities.

External Guidance

When you are practiced in listening to your external guidance system, your awareness of your contextual surroundings is heightened. You'll be able to hear the slight lilt at the end of your friend's statement about their supposed excitement over a weekend away. You'll be able to see how your husband closes his eyes while telling you about his day.

Maybe you'll notice the extra squeeze of a hug he gives you, like he wants to hold on a little longer. You'll notice the sound of your own hesitation in your voice and take a moment to yourself to dig a little deeper.

Building up these extra sensitivities can be tricky, especially if we aren't used to trusting our boundaries and strength in vulnerability. It's so much easier to sit and watch TV than to take 10 minutes to be silent and notice the sensations of exhaustion. It's so much easier to numb our sensitivities than to lean into them and learn to love them as the powerful skills that they are.

Intuition is a highly under-rated skill, but it can be so powerful to your bravery. Maybe you don't speak up and ask a hard question to your best friend with just one tiny lilt in her voice after a statement about her marriage. But if you've been listening to the external guidance around you and the internal guidance within you, then maybe you'll recognize that this wasn't the first lilt you've heard from her. Maybe it's time to speak up? Or maybe it's time to wait? Building a confidence in your intuitive skills will help find those answers.

Those answers will likely inform where the tension and resistance in the moment exists. This brings us to another component of improvisation: friction. When our intuition can highlight the friction, we don't have to receive that information as a dead end, but instead we can learn to lean on and use the friction to move forward in a moment of bravery.

Friction

Before we go any further, let's talk some more about Resonance.

Resonance is the quality of sound in an object when the vibration around it forces that object to sympathetically vibrate. Resonance requires friction and friction requires constraints. Friction and constraints are required to make music.

Think about an opera singer in front of a wine glass. If she sings with enough force at a frequency matching the mass of the wine glass, the glass will begin to vibrate sympathetically. And if she's using enough volume, that vibration cannot be contained by the laws of physics. Eventually it will shatter. That is resonance, albeit rather violent resonance.

Resonance from friction doesn't only happen in the physical world. It is written all over our most powerful moments in life. A surprise touchdown at a football game, an arena full of Adele fans singing (and crying) along with her lyrics, witnessing your dad cry for the first time, witnessing the birth of your child. These moments are so big, so powerful, that we have no choice but to have some sort of emotion alongside it. In those moments we are the wine glass compelled to move.

Even between two unsuitable, disharmonious elements, there is still resonance. It's subtle, but when your husband/wife/roommate leaves their socks everywhere and it irks you, it causes a dissonance within you. Dissonance is the tension between two objects or musical notes that lack harmony. Here's the catch, even within dissonance, there is still resonance.

In really simple terms, place two objects in a room and add enough friction/force somewhere in there and you'll hear resonance from all the vibrations.

Even more specific, let's talk about the cello. I know people may say they love the sounds the cello makes. Yes, the resonance from this instrument can be beautiful. But most likely, they haven't heard what a cello sounds like with too much or not enough friction between the bow and string. That kind of resonance is down right painful to hear.

At times it is musically appropriate to play the instrument in these ways, and to be honest I've played more recording sessions than I'd care to admit where the producer requests the very elusive 'rawness.' I know he's asking for either the gritty, angsty sound of too much friction or the pithy, scratchy, ghostly sound of not enough friction which I (and many other string players) spent years and years and years learning how to *avoid* creating.

Their request always makes me chuckle, not because I don't think that sound is suitable for the song we are currently working on (it always end up sounding great) but I find it hilarious to have spent 75 percent of my life learning how to not create that sound, only to get paid to create it.

I love dichotomies, and especially this one because as it turns out, the exact amount of experience I have in avoiding those sounds is a qualification to being a professional player of those god-awful sounds. (Let that one sink in for a bit.) If we use that as metaphor, then the friction we feel at the heights and depths of a season of life is practice for how to avoid or choose those feelings on purpose in the future.

Most of the time these tones from the cello are far from ideal because the amount of friction outweighs the quality of tone within the instrument, or vice versa—resulting in a thin, scratchy resonance. In order to make the luscious, mellow, and soaring sounds everyone loves from a cello—it takes an acute awareness of the friction being created on the string. To be aware of this friction takes an understanding of it, an extensive experience (failing) with it, and an thorough knowledge of it and its surroundings. (Oh, and a steady hand.)

As with the cello, if we are to resonate as humans we must be sensitive to the amount of friction in our lives and learn to use it. This friction is not a bad thing. Quite the opposite, when friction exists it means there is life and pent-up potential. It can be thrilling and terrifying to sense the onset of friction in our lives, but when we know how to fluently exist within that friction, we can handle it.

Friction presents itself as fear, hope, possibility, and expectation. How, you ask? Sense what happens inside you when you read the following sentences...

Scene: You just got an email. Your mom/dad is coming into town next week.

Scene: You're waiting in the theater wings to give a speech.

Scene: You're waiting to go into the conference room for a job interview.

Scene: Your pregnant sister has been in labor for over 24 hours.

Scene: You're driving 50 miles per hour. The traffic light ahead just turned from green to yellow.

Scene: The phone rings; it's your ex.

In all of these situations, you're either bracing yourself for dissonance, getting ready to have a great time, or proceed as normal. Either way, there's an expectation of a measure of resonance on the other side of every moment. To a degree, THAT is also imagination at work.

Using constraints, as with playing the cello, comes with a need to listen to and become intimately familiar with the friction (aka what the limitations demand of us) if we are to one day use them with skill, fluency, and intuition. A musician's experience in using these constraints results in the music we all know, love, and hate.

Becoming well-practiced in how this friction in life contributes to our lives, can be the difference between turning into bridezilla or enjoying your wedding day. When we become aware of this friction, we can then choose how to use it.

Power of Choice

"You can't be that kid standing at the top of the waterslide, overthinking it. You have to go down the chute."—Tina Fey

After acknowledging what your intuition is telling you about the friction, what next? Well, you can sit there and over-plan and over-analyze your next move. Or your can act, and *do* the thing.

In economics, the law of diminishing returns states "in all productive processes, adding more of one factor of production, while holding all others constant, will at some point yield lower incremental per-unit returns." In English, this means that at some point, adding more planning, worrying, and analyzing will eventually result in less than ideal outcomes. In Tina Fey's analogy (seen in the quote above) this could mean you waited so long to go down the waterslide that the water park closes.

The same principle works with caffeine and how much of it helps your productivity. If you live, like I do, in the Pacific Northwest then it's pretty standard for one shot of espresso to barely open your eyes. A second shot might perk up your productivity, but a third or a fourth might give you heart palpitations or an anxiety attack.

Power of choice and the law of diminishing returns play a role in bravery too. If you're standing at the other end of your junior high hallway mustering up the courage to ask the girl to the dance, there will come a moment when you have to take a step forward, clear your throat and allow the words to come out of your mouth. The timing and method of these actions is all wrapped up in power of choice.

When we are aware of this choice, it is dynamic. In fact, expert negotiators say that when you retain the ability to walk away from the deal, you also retain the power in the negotiation. Conversely, the negotiating party that feels obligated or feels the need to make some sort of deal work has given up part of its negotiating power.

Improvising doesn't solely occur in a boardroom while negotiating for custody rights of children. It also happens when you find yourself in a moment of brief terror while talking with a stranger at a networking party or in the dairy section of the grocery store when you see your kid's teacher.

For any improvisational situation of bravery, I love and abide by the rules of improvisation that Tina Fey outlines in her book, *Bossypants*, which is a hilarious read, by the way. If there's anyone we should trust about making the most of a situation with somewhat out-of-control factors, it's someone with the experience of Saturday Night Live.

Rules of Improvisation

Rule 1. AGREE. This task requires the honesty to acknowledge that you don't have total and complete control of the outcome of the situation. It is the acknowledgement that you are choosing to step into this moment with your full power of choice. In a musical improvisation this is the equivalent of picking up your instrument. Example: if a drummer opts out of this rule, she halts the forward momentum and groove of the improvisation. To be clear, you don't have to *agree* with the situation. You can agree to engage with an improvisational moment without agreeing to its current state of being. This rule is simply asking for a commitment to engage with all factors involved.

Rule 2. Say YES, AND. When you're in the midst of improvisation, contribute to the moment not by merely saying "yes" but by also adding to that "yes." Another example: If I were a cellist joining in with an improvisational piece with a drummer, saying "yes" might look like only making rhythmic sounds that mimic and go along with the drummer. Saying "yes AND" might look like making rhythmic sounds that also incorporate melody and harmonies. You're committing to add something of your own. This is also really great first date advice because from personal experience, when you're the only one in the conversation who is actually carrying the conversation, it's pretty tiring. If both parties are contributing to the conversation, it will naturally go smoother and easier, even if the date still turns out to be a dud.

Rule 3. MAKE STATEMENTS. This third rule of improvisation ensures that we are not only contributing to the moment, but we are dousing it with fuel to move forward as fast as possible. Rather than running around a networking party asking only questions to your peers, try making a few statements too. You'll notice that the statements allow the other parties involved in the improvisation to settle into the moment rather than feel like they're being interviewed for some newspaper article.

For example: If I spent an hour just following the lead of a drummer in an improvisational piece, even by adding melody and harmonies, the drummer and I would probably lose some steam and focus. "Making a statement" in this scenario might look like guiding a tempo change or a key change or hold onto your hats, inviting a new player to join us on stage! In essence "making a statement" is the choice to lead the movement into new opportunities.

Rule 4. THERE ARE ONLY OPPORTUNITIES. This is my favorite rule of improvisation. In an acting scenario, this is founded upon the belief that two actors are better than one or rather, "My contributions and ideas are infinitely more vast when I combine them with yours." It's also the recognition that the friction within a given moment is not the problem, it is part of the solution.

This rule applies to bravery in this way: if we can recognize our fear as part of friction, then we know that regardless of how we use our fear, our fear is part of creating opportunities.

If you allow the fear to victimize your circumstances then you've chosen those subsequent opportunities. Choosing to enter into a set of environmental constraints is not inherently a mistake, because those limitations provide you with a set of choices & opportunities. On a road trip, the choice to *not* fill the car with gasoline will eventually give you a new set of opportunities: hitch hike, call AAA, cry on the side of the road. Your situation might require all three options!

Turning Victimization Into Your Power of Choice

Finding your power of choice in a given moment can be some of the toughest seasons you'll go through because there's something so exhausting and all-consuming about the feeling of victimization. Those of us who *have* been legitimately victimized, our power of choice remains. It resides in the response and reaction we have to that moment and every following moment.

Ask yourself these questions to uncover your power of choice when you've been feeling like you've lost it all.

- Which parts of this situation did I not choose?
- If any, which parts of this situation did I choose?
- If I had a magic wand to wave over this, how would things go differently from today onward?
- Now, without making excuses for or trying to protect those who victimized me, how am I choosing to remain in this state of consciousness?

Let me be absolutely clear: I make no argument for who is to blame or how badly it all sucks when our boundaries have been trampled on. This is not an attempt to dull the pain of feeling like our external limitations are squeezing the life out of our throats. Victimization is serious business.

In spite of all their darkness, these moments of victimization retain their shape of opportunity to improvise. These improvisational opportunities are not asking you to abandon blame, justice, or your decorum, sanity, and sense of safety. Nope. Quite the opposite. These opportunities are calling upon our sense of dignity, pride, and respect for ourselves. This internal sense of "No, I will not let you treat me that way." is an invitation to build our bravery. Conveniently, that's what we unfold in the next chapters.

Part Three

How to Build Your Bravery

"It doesn't happen all at once,' said the Skin Horse. 'You become. It takes a long time. That's why it doesn't happen often to people who break easily, or have sharp edges, or who have to be carefully kept. Generally, by the time you are Real, most of your hair has been loved off, and your eyes drop out and you get loose in the joints and very shabby. But these things don't matter at all, because once you are Real you can't be ugly, except to people who don't understand." —Margery Williams Bianco, The Velveteen Rabbit

"Life shrinks or expands in proportion to one's courage."— Anaïs Nin

My favorite architect is Gaudi. Yes, the aesthetic of his body of work is unique and widely appreciated. But I'm particularly drawn to him for one specific piece of he left for us to enjoy, his Basílica i Temple Expiatori de la Sagrada Família, or simply Barcelona's Sagrada Família.

A Barcelona bookseller, Josep Maria Boccabella returned from a trip to Italy with the inspiration to start building a church. Construction on this church began in 1882 and a year later Gaudi stepped into the project and radically changed the design.

You should see this thing. It's huge. In fact, it's so huge, that when Gaudi died in 1926 the project was only 15 percent complete. He worked on and visioned this project for 43 years and only got to see one of the 18 spires completed. Construction is still not complete.

I repeat, over a century has passed and the construction is still not complete.

OVER. ONE. HUNDRED. YEARS.

This creative endeavor has survived fires, civil wars, world wars, more fires, modern transportation problems, city planning, hosting the Olympics, and who knows what else might happen in the final years of construction!

Parts of this project would not have even been feasible without today's modern construction practices and technology. Yet still he designed it. Gaudi was most likely walking around the construction site telling people, "That last set of massive spires? Don't worry about it. You'll figure it out eventually." In fact he is quoted saying, "My client is not in a hurry."

Construction on this Spanish darling of a building is expected to finish in the first third of the 21st century. I hope they celebrate on a new moon, when the sky is its darkest because fireworks always look best under the darkest skies.

Fireworks always get me thinking about the pyrotechnician in charge. The guy holding that "big red button." It must feel pretty epic because lighting the night sky does not take much more than pushing the right button.

Gaudi's foresight and fortitude to envision all that an idea could become—if given enough time, manpower, expertise, technology, and support—is worthy of goosebumps. I get them sitting here at my desk in the Pacific Northwest 133 years after he caught the vision. Oh, and then he had the audacity to act on it.

I get goosebumps because I can't help but envision the Sagrada Familia as a metaphor for Bare Naked Bravery.

Do we have the fortitude and foresight to envision our lives with courageous creativity? Are we giving ourselves enough time, enough manpower, enough social "technology," and support? Are we willing to step outside a timeline?

You already have it in you.

All that you've experienced has brought you to this point.

You have everything you need to take the next step, however minuscule or massive it seems.

Is Bravery Born or Built?

If you build the skills of using vulnerability, imagination, and improvisation on a daily basis your overall Bravery will build. There's no way it couldn't. Your value of self-care, mindful observation, internal strength, and faith to take action on these skills will overflow beyond conceptual and into real areas of your life. This practice of building bravery will translate to being fluent in the language of Bare Naked Bravery. It's impossible for it not to.

We practice to make it easier, not perfect.

After all, a bucket of rainwater is just a collection of tiny raindrops.

The most magical moments I've experienced as a musician are in the ending of a song. Not just any song, but those that consume me. It happens in the performances (or even practice sessions) where I have no brain capacity reserved for acknowledging anyone else in the room. All my energy is aimed at listening to the music, observing my body, attuning my ear to the surrounding notes, and sensing the flow of the song's story.

I've seen it happen to other performers, so I know I'm not the only one. The artist finishes the last note of the song, looks up from their instrument, in that instant you can tell they forgot about the audience. They are back from a musical vortex and have magically reappeared on stage.

Another not-so-public version of this magic is looking up from the desk, guitar, computer, piano, canvas and realizing that not just one hour has passed, but FIVE hours. And oh yeah, your stomach is growling and you have to pee. You've time-traveled yourself through the process of creation.

These are the sweet spots of practice.

In this section, I'd like to introduce you to my favorite methods of practicing daily bravery. Building the skill of being vulnerable, imaginative, and improvisational doesn't come overnight. Acknowledging these little spurts of daily bravery enhances the magic of Bare Naked Bravery. You'll soon find yourself reaching into new corners of courage to assist in your making the world a better place.

Even the act of intentionally setting aside time to practice your bravery is brave! It takes a radically indulgent and defiant act of self-care to reserve a 10- to 15-minute block of time to write unabashedly. It's a bold thing to stop everything to sit still for 20 minutes practicing your intuition. It takes strength to put all your uncensored self on the page, even if it's just a flabbergasted list of exhaustion. It's an act of faith to throw your journal pages in the fireplace, trusting that tomorrow you will have more words to fill the page.

5 Characteristics & 5 Gifts of Practicing Bravery Building

1: Curiosity

While practicing your bravery, the magical time travel I mentioned earlier might look like following a "white rabbit" of curiosity. Following this white rabbit of curiosity takes you beyond the land of fear. You are no longer scared of the unknown, but instead lost within the presence and practice of curiosity and bravely, too!

For example, what would the potluck be like if you brought the most absurdly ridiculous casserole instead of reaching the level of perfection fear is holding you to? Maybe this gets your fingers to start listing out the most absurd ingredient list ever known to man? Maybe this provokes a memory? Maybe it unearths a distaste for artichoke hearts which reveals an overall displeasure of varying textures?

By infusing curiosity into your bravery building you'll start to notice the sting of the unknown will subside. Instead you'll find yourself lost within the presence and practice of curiosity and doing it bravely, too!

While building bravery, using the phrase "I wonder…" and asking any question is a great trigger for this transformation into curiosity. This is precisely why I've included the resources in your book bonuses and in the back of the book. (Download your book bonuses here: http://emilyannpeterson.com/bnb-book)

A Side-note About Creative Leaks

Before I eliminated caffeine from my diet in an effort to minimize the shaking in my hand, I was a devout coffee drinker. But there was a crack in the coffee pot at my house and I resented every drop it left behind… for two reasons:

1. That was a drop of coffee that could've been in my cup.

2. Sooner or later someone was going to have to clean that up. I'm strong breed of a grumpy morning person—(we do exist)—so starting the day by reminding me of all the cleaning I should be doing is NOT the ideal.

Creativity leaks are going to happen. If you are diligent in your observation of daily bravery building, you will begin to see the 'drips' appear on your mental countertop space.

Creativity leaks can look like:

- Forgetting to change the oil in the car.
- Remembering that thing he said years ago.

- That silly electrical cord getting in the way.
- Getting kicked off the internet repeatedly.
- Those reports due at the end of the week.
- Lovely interruptions at a neighborhood coffeeshop.
- Forgetting something you need to do for the business trip next weekend.
- Not hearing from a family member in a long time.

We can't avoid the existence of creativity leaks. There will be a leak somewhere. We can prevent or even remove some of the them, but it takes an observer's mentality to notice when the drip on the mental-countertop space looks familiar.

During your practice of bravery I urge you to keep an eye out for the leaking of your fearful heart. Observe the dripping worry. Observe how much effort you waste in reacting to "dropping the ball" or flat-out failure. Just observe and notice, no judgment necessary.

Who knows? Maybe you'll get frustrated enough to either metaphorically get some duct tape to plug the leak or better yet find an extra $5 to buy a new coffeepot from Goodwill.

2: (Un)censored

When growing up a teenager in Texas, a precociously outspoken little 5-year-old neighbor girl who would invite herself over for dinners at our house. The doorbell would ring and I would open up to find a little head of white-blonde hair standing only as tall as the doorknob.

Kelsey would usually say something like, "Oh Hi! Can I come in?" while walking in, of course.

I loved that kid.

And she loved butter.

Boy, did she love butter.

She would spread butter on bread like it was humanity's last chance to enjoy the combination of gluten and fat in a single bite. She was more than generous with that butter and knife, and oh, so messy. It got on her face, her fingers, the table, the plate— there was butter everywhere. She practically glistened by the end of the whole thing. It was beautiful.

Her abandonment of what others thought of her was my favorite part. She was completely oblivious to the looks of horror from the adults in the dining room. Even if she did notice, she wouldn't have cared. It was so punk rock. I admired her, and I admired her radical acts of uncensored indulgence.

Here I was in high school, completely consumed (to the point of mental illness) by what those same adults thought of me. I would analyze my behaviors and calorie intake like a cow chews its cud. I was hyper alert to the glances of "Are you sure you want that second scraping of butter on your bread?" I was completely lost in worry and anxiety, I could hardly see straight.

Fear had me by the collar and I was owned by it. Not so with this kid. We later found out she was coming to our house while her mom was making *their* family meal. Let's just say she knew how to butter both sides of the bread.

You see, fear is from the land of not enough time and too fast. Fear is from a land of imbalance, too dangerous, too poor, too overwhelmed, too scarce, too much, too many, and not enough.

Fear is a roller coaster. In an instant it can swing our freelance calendars from "I'm way too busy and can't take on any more projects" all the way to "Crap. No one needs me! How am I going to pay rent?" I have personally experienced the terror of "Wait. What?! I thought things were going to be all right yesterday!" only to have one small detail change and floods of relief (or terror) and peaceful (or fitful) nights of sleep rush in (or vanish.)

So how does this practice of bravery help when life is handing us constraint after constraint after constraint?

I hear you. Fostering creative abundance seems utterly ridiculous when we're smack in the midst of fear. However, the more we practice getting to the freedom and abundance of uncensored expression, the easier it is to access in the future. Maya Angelou was right about creativity, "The more you use, the more you have." That sentiment equally applies to Bravery and the freedom of expression it requires.

There will always be enough creativity to go around. As we discussed earlier, creativity begets courage. Thusly, there will always be enough courage. It will arrive through your curious observation in the midst of fear. It will arrive on its own abundant terms of time and resources.

Allow it to happen. Don't stand in the way of it. Don't try to muscle it down or out.

Let your expression be like Kelsey-The-Kid. Butter both sides of the bread. Get the butter everywhere.

3: Frequency

"Great acts are made up of small deeds."—*Lao Tzu*

If I asked you to lie on the floor of a room for 5 minutes alone, the constant thinking, thinking, thinking your brain would do uses the narrative part of your brain. "I wonder how long I'll be here. What's going on in the other room? I wonder what I'll have for lunch tomorrow." Those kind of thoughts light up an intricate and vast web of regions in our brain.

Neurologists call this the Default Mode Network, or DMN. It's the web of self-referencing, memories, judgments, social concepts, stories about the past, wishes for the future and just general mind-wandering. This is the portion of our brain we engage when we're anxious and fear-based narrative tapes play in our heads.

However the Insula Cortex region of the brain doesn't have a linear, time-based narrative like the DMN. This is the part of the brain that lights up like fireworks when someone is skilled in the practice of mindfulness, zen-like focus and observation.

Here's the cool part: when someone skilled in the practice of mindfulness or zen-like focus lights up this Insula Cortex portion of the brain, conversely the Default Mode Network decreases in activity. This means if your daily practice is filled with mindfulness, meditative, zen-like focus and curious observation, it is shown to decrease the narrative tapes of anxiety.

The more you practice 'turning on' your Insula Cortex, the easier it becomes to 'turn off' your DMN.

Mic drop

How bout them apples?! This is the beauty of a stream-of-consciousness writing practice and meditation. It lets your "monkey brain" out on the page and encourages the zen-like mindfulness to surface. Go without judgment and notice with curiosity. Sit in the discomfort, write through it, and watch it pass.

And here's what's really awesome: whatever you repeat, gets easier to repeat in the future.

This is where the frequency of your daily bravery building comes into play. By exploring your bravery daily in this way, you are building the skill of lighting up the Insula Cortex regions of your brain and turning off the Default Mode Network.

The more you access and use your Insula Cortex, the easier it is to do in the future. This fact is unavoidable.

Earlier we talked about how and why bravery is contagious. Remember that every neuron in our brain is connected to other neurons through synapses and those connections get stronger through strengthening the myelin around each synapse. I like to think of myelin as a tiny, long, sticky piece of tape wrapped around and around the synapses we practice the most.

This myelin is created through repetition of a behavior, act, or thought. The more we repeat something, the more myelin gets wrapped around those synapses required to accomplish the repetition. In turn, those synapses are stronger and easier for our brain to access.

Musicians are great examples of this. Successfully playing a particular set of fingerings and bowings just once might be extremely difficult. But successfully repeating this same difficult passage of music at least 10 times in a row automatically implies that this same passage is now exponentially easier. After 10 repetitions, perhaps the passage of music is not the easiest it will ever be, but it's easier nonetheless.

Repetition of any task builds myelin around the synapses required to do that task. The more myelin there is, the easier it is to repeat that task, thought, or behavior.

This is just the fact of practice: We practice to make things easier.

A lack of myelin is one of the main reasons a stroke victim has re-learn how to talk, eat, or walk. They are re-building the myelin around tender, damaged neurons. (The brain is a miracle and I could talk about it for days.)

So regardless of how impermanent our practice of bravery is, the more often we repeat the practice, the stronger our access to Bare Naked Bravery becomes.

Because by learning to observe our daily expression, over time we can begin to discover just how hard we work to fight against or ignore our constraints instead of using them. Even the act of remembering how impermanent fear is (ex: trashing your writing) will get easier with every day you practice it.

So how often? And for how long?

During seasons of great constraint, partaking in some Bravery Building practices multiple times each day might be best. During my own bouts of depression, sometimes I have had to sit down to write three to seven times every day. Other times 10 minutes of meditation is all you'll need to find your courage and watch the sandcastle of fear melt under the impermanence of your thoughts. When you have the luxury of time, practicing bravery building for up to 2 hours might even feel necessary on some days.

On the days when your life is a bright and shiny pile of unicorn glitter and doesn't remotely resemble Eeyore's little storm cloud, even on those days expression is a great place to observe your gratitude and observation of thanksgiving.

Over time and with practice you might begin to notice a need to write or be silent a little bit before a difficult phone call or after a strange conversation.

So how often and for how long should you practice building bravery? Feel it out. Practice using your intuition on that. *wink* Let your constraints and your ingredients of bravery answer that question throughout your practice.

Just know that once is not going to cut it. One step does not equal a mile. One drop does not equal a bucketful. You'll begin to notice the benefits of frequent impermanence when it is a daily practice, not a special snowflake event.

4: Fluency

Pick the right tools.

If you're using your strengths (not your weaknesses) to practice then your fluency will play a big role in your practice of building bravery. The right set of tools can make all the difference in the world. I'll go more in depth with my own favorite tools to practice bravery in the next chapters, but I suggest exploring them all with curiosity to find the ones that feels most "fluent."

The benefit of using tools of fluency is that your practice of bravery will also feel fluent and easy too. We want this.

There is a time and a place to stretch yourself into practicing bravery with non-fluent tools, but even the acknowledgment that a method of practice isn't quite "fluent" yet will help the experience.

Pro-tip: Allow your strengths to lead your practice.

As adults, it's easy to forget what it feels like to be a total noob at something. Being the new kid on the block is not an experience that most of us lean into with glee. In fact, some of us haven't done anything completely new since the days of kindergarten.

Ahh, kindergarten, the giver of all life skills. Everything after that terrifyingly exciting day of education has only been an addition. Little did we know then, but those days of crayons and lunch boxes were training wheels for teamwork/relational skills and coloring inside (or outside) the lines.

Remember what it felt like to be totally new? Bumbling about with crayons? Unsteady on the playground? Unsure of where the bathroom was?

In the last couple of years, I've done some pretty new things, but even I'll admit they were skills merely built upon the older ones, the skills I already had.

- Yes, I totally butchered my first attempt at a little felted sheep at my friend's studio—but I had at least 30 years of hand-eye coordination and several childhood years of working with hobby clay (which began in kindergarten.) The second attempt at a sheep didn't turn out half-bad.

- Yes, I picked up a couple of new instruments in the last couple years. No, I'm not *great* at them. But I've been listening to, singing along and studying music my whole life. So it's not surprising (to me at least) to be a cellist turned singer/songwriter who now dabbles in a little piano, ukulele, and guitar. It's like picking up a new color of crayon. (Perhaps you have your own version of these crayons?)

- Yes, I might've gotten lost on the way to a new house-sitting gig last weekend, but it certainly wasn't my first night with a driver's license. I got there, eventually. Just like I eventually found the restroom in the elementary school.

- Yes, I might've "lost" a sale with a potential consulting client, but it certainly wasn't the first conversation I had had with a human. No one died or lost a friend. In fact, I might've made a friend!

The stepping stones of practicing bravery are made of your strengths. These steps are built upon the blocks we've already strengthened. Practicing Bare Naked Bravery requires the use of these strengthened blocks.

When you practice anything with the mindset of "leading with strength," it becomes easier to transform fear into curiosity and soon after, more bravery. It's even better when these transformation skills are practiced often on little moments of bravery, like daily writing or meditations. Over time it becomes easier to diffuse the bigger moments (first date jitters, first day on the job, first song of the performance, first sentence of the public speech, etc.) into smaller moments of curiosity.

Focusing on something you're actually good at bolsters your confidence to stand strong even within the limitations of your constraints. Allowing strengths to lead your Curiosity does not promise to remove the constraint of inexperience or "weakness." Instead, this practice of allowing strength to lead calls us to use constraints in a way that feels more comfortable than allowing our weakness to lead curiosity.

Conversely, allowing your weakness to lead your practice of bravery might sound like...

"God, why are you such an idiot?"
"How come you always choose the most inopportune times to make your comments?"
"Wow. So much ignorance coming out of your mouth?"

That doesn't sound like a fun brain to spend a lot of time in, does it? Allowing our strengths to lead the curiosity maintains a solid ground of comfortable habits and routines while strengthening and stretching our bravery. Doing it this way means we get to confidently find curious novelty and newness rather than berate ourselves into fear-filled exploration.

5: (Im)permanence

Impermanence within your practice of bravery has a threefold purpose.

1) Impermanence is a reminder of safety.

When I tell folks I delete my daily writing and expression, I am often met with a horrified look and perhaps a question like, "But what if you write something awesome? You're just going to trash it?" I've been doing this enough to know that if my writing is truly good, I'll be able to recreate it, but better with intention.

The extra work to recreate something pales in comparison to the sense of safety required to build my bravery. Even the hint of potentially keeping my writing is enough to usher in a tidal wave of censorship. (ex: "What if someone finds this journal after I died and thinks I'm an asshole for saying that?!") Ain't nobody got time for that!

Keeping the impermanence of my bravery building sacred is necessary. To some degree, impermanence is the thorny, protective part of the "pine cone" of practicing bravery. Starting fresh every day ensures my attempts remain in a nurturing sanctuary for my bravery.

This might mean the blank page becomes your beacon of safety. Deleting, burning, or trashing your daily writing means no one will read it later. Not even you. It might look like doing one of the same five guided meditations every day. It might mean scheduling your practice of bravery in the early morning hours to give your future self a fresh start. However it looks, impermanence provides tomorrow with the same fresh slate, the same chance to explore within the same safety.

2) Practicing impermanence is a reminder that everything is temporary, even fear.

On the days when daily the practice of bravery contains a seemingly endless list of fears, throwing your pages of writing into the fire or into your computer's trash bin is a wonderful reminder that everything is temporary. Knowing that tomorrow will hold another chance can fill you with such relief. Reminders of impermanence are especially welcome at the end of a fitful and distracted meditation of mine.

Maybe this looks like starting your meetings with an accountability partner or connection group with a ritual of acknowledging this impermanence. Perhaps this looks like lighting a candle at the start of the meeting and blowing it out at the end. Or maybe this reminder of impermanence is throwing out yesterday's to-do list every morning.

Leaving space for impermanence within your daily practice of bravery is a reminder that we are the ones with the control over what matters and what lasts; promising that the fear's grip on life will last only as long as we allow. No one says, you have to keep the page containing all your written fears. Throw that sucker into the fireplace!

3) Impermanence is a reminder of potential.

The act of making a clean start is never easy. It always seems to involve something like deep cleaning the bathroom (gross) or culling through your closet (ugh) or breaking up with someone (ouch). But the extra effort to ensure a blank slate can really pay off.

Starting from scratch can be tough ... but exhilarating. There's something so exciting about a clean start. It's exhilarating because with that fresh start, we acknowledge the potential in the space we've created. Deleting or trashing your writing every day is a ritual of a blank slate for tomorrow. Acts like throwing out yesterday's to-do list every morning, immediately grants yourself a second (and third and thirty-third) chance to nurture the space for your potential.

After practicing bravery with a character of impermanence, you begin to rely on the blank page as a symbol of hope for tomorrow's fresh start.

It's because of these three reasons that I'll venture to say that leaving room for impermanence in your daily practice of bravery might be the most radical act of defiant expectation in existence. Even though that day's practice lasts for a short amount of time, the practice of creating space for courage tomorrow is an investment. Believe me, it's worth it.

When we incorporate impermanence, fluency, frequency, freedom from censorship and curiosity into our daily practices of bravery, we automatically make room for the gifts that this kind of practice brings. Of course these gifts are not the sole reason why we practice bravery. Remember we practice bravery to make bravery easier. However, these are some of my favorite bonus side-effects from this kind of daily practice.

The 5 Gifts Found Within a Practice of Building Bravery

1) Self-care.

(Win!) Ignoring the effects of constraints on our life is in essence ignoring ourselves. Therefore a practice of bravery that includes honesty means we are acknowledging how our constraints affect us. That is self-care.

Even if it's as simple as saying "Oh no!" after spilling the milk, that exclamation is the honest acknowledgment about your situation. Identifying the honesty is an acknowledgment of loss or disappointment.

Practicing that kind of honesty in the midst of trying circumstances is practicing bravery. Doing this kind of mindful practice heightens our sensitivity to how life affects us. Tadah! We are caring for ourselves.

2) Permission to be imperfect.

(Win!) In its purest form practice is not meant to be perfect. If your daily bravery practice involves writing, then I bet you aren't writing the next great American novel. Quite the opposite.

Censorship is just another constraint! By releasing expectations for our practice of bravery to be/ do/stand up to whatever our constraints demand from us, we are also finding freedom from those expectations (even if it's temporary and expressed to only yourself). Practicing bravery releases us from the immediate constraints of the moment.

3) A chance to discover what could be.

(Win!) Even if your constraints are contributing to less than ideal circumstances, by highlighting "what is" you are simultaneously providing an opportunity to acknowledge "what could be." Unless you identify your observations of the way things are, there will be less hope for better things to come.

Maybe your daily practice of bravery reveals all the ways your spouse has failed you. This grievous list is a twisted way of identifying the way you'd *prefer* things to be, a way things could be different. When you're at such a loss of what to do and where to go, you have to start somewhere. Daily practices of bravery help you find that place.

On the heels of highlighting "what is," our intuition steps in to make suggestions for ways to make "what could be" happen.

4) A chance to sense the next steps.

(Win!) Maybe your daily practice of bravery unveils a really long list of obligations. You might not think that being honest about "Get more milk from the grocery store" gives you any insight. I beg to differ.

Example: Although not the most artsy-fartsy thing our hands will create, writing an uncensored to-do list will release your brain from holding and keeping track of responsibilities. *cough cough CONSTRAINTS cough* The gift provided to us from this kind of practice is that we can now have the 'brain space' to decide how and when to accomplish those items.

Practicing bravery daily gives us space to listen to our improvisation, intuition and power of choice rather than get caught up in the chaos of lack of clarity.

5) Hope.

It might not seem like it at first, but there is hope found in practicing bravery, because it prompts the immediate practice of using our constraints. We can find the clarity of mind to decide our next steps. When we intentionally practice this we are practicing the knowledge that our improvisational skills and intuition will provide us with our next steps—this is hope. We are not confined by a lack of power with a daily practice of bravery, instead we get more and more intimately acquainted with our power of choice and intuitive sense of timing to move forward with vulnerability and a vision of possibility.

Just imagine the source of strength we can find from this hope when our practice of expression is intentional and daily!

Putting It All Out There

As with becoming fluent in anything, the practicing of bravery does not have shortcuts. If they existed, those shortcuts would only bite you in the ass later. The practice of using the ingredients mentioned in earlier chapters is done over a long period of dedication, attention, repetition, failure, and acute observation.

So, sorry, there's no shortcut to building bravery.

But! Good news!

1) There is no deadline.

No one's out there claiming that by the time you're a certain age you should have certain amount of bravery built to handle life. So go ahead and relieve yourself of any deadline you might be holding over yourself. Don't be so mean (to yourself and possibly others) by enforcing imaginary deadlines.

2) Small choices add up.

When you make the choice to build up your bravery, please know that it is a practice of valiant attempts and valiant failures. Each of them adds up to become the strength of courage your future self will appreciate some day.

Not only that, but you never know. Sometimes mundane choices have magical outcomes. Let's drive this point home with some Disney. Because why the hell not? [Insert my own feminist uproar here.]

Okay, okay. I mean, we're all aware how unreal fairytales are, but we're equally aware of how fantastical they are. So in the name of the fantastical imagination required for Bravery, here is just one handful of stories beginning with small, mundane choices.

- Belle chose to look for her father in the woods.
- The kids chose to listen to bedtime stories about Neverland.
- Snow White chose to eat an apple.
- Sleeping Beauty chose to mess around with a spinning wheel.
- Aladdin chose a lamp.
- Pongo the Dalmatian went on a walk with Roger, his owner.
- Ariel chose to again disobey her father and go to the ocean surface.

When added up, small choices to just keep going and keep trying can have unintended and magical implications. Even beyond fairy tale stories we see this truth in real life, too.

- Walt Disney was fired from a newspaper for "not having enough imagination or good ideas" and then went on to fail at business more than once before he stumbled on a little cartoon creation named Mickey.

- Beatrix Potter's precious children's book was rejected so many times she self-published 250 copies. It has now sold 45 million.

- Henry Ford's failed business attempts left him broke at least five times until he started Ford Motor Company

- [Skipping list of every Olympic medal winner for brevity]

- The manager of the Grand Ole Opry fired Elvis Presley after just one performance telling him, "You ain't goin' nowhere, son. You ought to go back to drivin' a truck."

- Oprah was fired from her job at a television station because she was "unfit for TV."

- Five years before her novels exploded, the beloved J.K. Rowling was a broke, severely depressed, recently divorced, single mom attending school and getting her manuscripts repeatedly rejected.

It takes multiple attempts to make something great out of seemingly nothing much. Bare Naked Bravery, though present in us all, might take some practice for it to succeed like you want it to.

Recently, a marketing client of mine was comparing her business growth to her competitors. Her business was just barely a year old, while her competitors had been around for close to a decade. This mindset of comparison had worked herself into considering abandoning ship altogether.

I told her this: If you walked up to any baby and screamed in its face 'You're a terrible excuse for a human!' I would slap you immediately for being an asshole. It's a baby! The poor thing is doing everything it can to be everything it needs to survive and you're over there yelling at it to "Be a better baby!' Are you kidding me? Not cool, babe. Not cool.

So if your vulnerability isn't very vulnerable or your honesty isn't very honest or maybe your imagination is as exciting as an entirely beige outfit, or perhaps your intuition is as fluid as a piece of steel, I beg you to not be hard on yourself. Those areas just need some nurturing. Let them be in their baby stage. Give them what they need to continue being everything they want to become.

Bravery Building Tools

Now that we've laid out the characteristics of and gifts from practicing bravery, in this chapter I'll introduce my favorite *tools* for practicing bravery. Please know that this is not an extensive list, merely my favorite methods of how I practice bravery on a regular basis.

I encourage you to get creative and use the previously mentioned characteristics of bravery building tools (curiosity, uncensorship, frequency, fluency, and impermanence) to create your own tools. Remember the goal is find the tools that foster those characteristics by giving you a chance to explore the depths of Bare Naked Bravery.

I don't care who you are. I don't care what you've been through. I don't care what fustercluck you're dealing with. The greatest gift I could give you is this: nurturing the bravery you already have. But I cannot give you this, try as I might. The choice to build upon your bravery cannot come from me. The most I can do for your courage lies in the remaining pages of this book.

I can give you the recipe, but at the end of the day, you'll be the one making the dinner.

So in the following chapters you'll receive the best tools for building bravery. Practicing bravery is meant to expose your vulnerability, enhance your imagination, and empower your improvisation. So get curious and try as many of these that strike your fancy and inspire your power of choice.

Bravery Building Tool #1: Expression

When I kept silent my soul wasted away…—Psalm 32

The first and most helpful tool for building bravery is daily expression or writing. Most days, this looks like stream-of-consciousness writing that I immediately delete or throw away.

This daily writing (and erasing of it) fosters the environment I need to really get to know all my timidness and hesitation and struggle. Doing this might look different for everyone. The goal is to sit down and write whatever comes to your mind in a way which allows observation. For me, that means I delete or trash it afterward.

The same elements of this daily writing habit nurture a highly similar environment as a fruitful music practice room or a highly productive business brainstorm session. If you're a dancer, you'll probably relate to this in your dance studio. If you're a hiker you might recognize a similar benefit from fresh air on top of a mountain. If you're a boxer, then the gym is your sandbox. If you're an actor, an empty rehearsal room is your sandbox.

They are all wonderful sandboxes: a low pressure, impermanent environment to explore new ideas fluently and without censorship.

What the hell is impermanent stream-of-consciousness writing?!

Quite a mouthful, huh? But it's fairly simple...

- Start from a blank slate, a blank page.
- Get it all out of your brain through writing.
- Curiously observe what unrolls without judgement.
- Finally, delete, trash, or burn what you just wrote.

The only objective with this kind of expression is to complete one repetition of the above cycle. There you have it.

It's like plugging a hose into your brain and letting the words spill out onto the page without any filter. It lets the most embittered thoughts out, all your obligated tasks unroll. It lets all the complaints and problems onto the page. It's like letting your fingers comb out all the fearful knots in your brain, or all the 'nots' (not enough, etc.)

Your daily pages of writing will be far from perfect. You're not trying to write a novel or memoir. I hope to God the pages aren't perfect because, ironically, those imperfect pages are perfect seeds for bravery. These pages foster space to be mindful, because then we have the space and presence of mind ripe with potential for what could be.

Some days the page will read like a bitchy list of to-do items and an 'I hate' list. Some days the writing will be inquisitive with a lot of questions and musings and 'what if's.' Some days the words will read as if Darkness itself reached for the page and smeared its sorrow and grief all over it. Oh and if overly judging yourself happens in your daily life, then it'll definitely happen on the page too.

If fear is your greatest nemesis, one of the many beauties of this daily practice of writing is that the page is a safe place to finally befriend the fear. After all, it's just a piece of paper - you're going to burn it later. It's just a measly .txt file - you're gonna delete it later.

It might not seem like it at first, but there is hope found in this practice of daily using constraints through expression.

By nurturing an environment for Bare Naked Bravery through this daily expression writing, we can infuse an element of safety into this new way of being brave. You see, expression takes the pressure out of the whole terrifying situation, because there is only one goal: Explore Bravery.

Write whatever comes to mind and vomit all the honesty onto the page with great abandon. It won't be pretty. Sometimes the sentences won't make sense. The goal is to fluently acknowledge the elements of your life that require honesty, risk, context, vision of possibility, defiant expectation, constraints, intuition, friction, and power of choice - Bare Naked Bravery.

How it all started...

This regular practice started as innocently as my 12-year-old self, with a daily "Dear Diary." Journaling every morning through my hopes, stresses, and complaints. I tore through blank notebooks and journals like a hungry omnivore at a Korean BBQ restaurant. Alongside this teenage daily writing, I also practiced music daily.

When my proficiency in both writing and music began to allow it... this expression occurred through music and became the outlet for that which I was not allowed to say out loud. There were opinions, stories, desires, lightness and darkness on the pages and hidden between the musical notes I played.

I kept writing words and playing music because I soon discovered that if I stopped the expression, I would stop living. From many angles, expression saved my life. I know I'm not the only one for whom this is true.

During seasons of great constraint expression through writing and music gave the seeds of my bravery a place to grow roots. My vulnerability, imagination, and improvisation found a space to expand and deepen when it wasn't very safe to do so outside of this daily expression.

Even though my shitty situations still hadn't changed, expression gave me a safe place to explore my Bare

Naked Bravery, by holding back the "demons," so I could catch my breath and regain my strength.

I know the practice of pure expression to be the best tool I have for building bravery, specifically impermanent stream-of-consciousness writing. It's is the best tool I can give you to mindfully begin to practice using your fear and harnessing the power of your constraints.

Why I Burned ALL My Journals

Throughout my unintentional hobby of collecting and using journals, I attended a couple of book clubs for artsy types. The most powerful, was going through *The Artist's Way* by Julia Cameron. (If you haven't gone through that book, I highly recommend it.) Part of her homework is what she calls "Morning Pages," daily stream-of-consciousness writing by hand on either 3 pages or for 30 minutes, whichever comes first every morning. Throughout the workbook you are to keep the stack of pages of morning writing and reference them occasionally during the book reading process.

While going through Cameron's book (several times) I began to morph my morning writing practice. Despite her admonition against it, I found that some days I did better typing. My fingers are better able to keep up with my brain's thoughts at that speed and I'm not killing trees in the process. I would spew my words on the page and then save the document in a folder on my laptop.

But I was still collecting it all. Countless computer files and notebook after notebook after notebook of journal writing. In fact the box in which I collected all my journals kept traveling with me to every new apartment and city. The box of journals was impressive, but dude. It was heavy, both figuratively and literally.

I couldn't continue carrying this box of journals around for forever. So, per the suggestion of a friend, one day I began to transfer 'the important stuff' into an electronic archive. What a great idea! I could take a stroll through memory lane and build an archive in the technology cloud and say goodbye to that dusty box of paper.

So I picked a journal at random.

FIVE hours later, I had the one journal archived and had acquired a brain-splitting migraine. I was exhausted. The archiving process only reminded me of terrible things people had said, feelings I had purged, and days of my life I had long forgotten. Some memories were fun to recall, and some were "warm fuzzies" for the soul, but generally I realized I had forgotten most of it, on purpose.

My subconscious had worked very hard to whitewash them from my mind. It did this not in avoidant way. But I realized the archiving process felt like leaving your own house with a suitcase-full of belongings, arriving back to your parents old house and trying to jam in an equivalent amount of clothing that no longer fit. Not necessarily impossible, but definitely unnecessary.

I knew I couldn't make it through 20-plus journals just like it. The archiving unearthed it all and I was no better for it.

Here's why: because the journal writing had already served its purpose. The practice of writing daily had given me a forum, a safe place. Those pages permitted me to lay out my insides and start the day from a stronger place. Those pages were the lenses that had allowed me to truly see myself in the present moment.

I didn't need to keep them. I didn't need the reminders and the bits and pieces didn't matter in the long run.

So the box of journals was brought outside and burned. I put them in a metal trash can and lit them on fire one by one. It took several hours of poking at the fire. Every once in a while, I could see a word on a burning page. Through the bonfire, those flashes of memory were enough of an archive for me.

The ashes went into the nearby river. It was time for the pages of words to move on. It was time to collect new words. Time to express new life and even let those new words move on and move me along.

I still write most days. Usually first thing in the morning. Sometimes it's not. Usually I write for 15 minutes, but sometimes a lot longer.

Two things have changed about my daily writing practice:

1. I write on anything: my phone's note app, a blank text document, a plain piece of paper, the back of an old bill.

2. When the writing comes to a close, I throw it away, immediately. I delete it. I rip up and I shred it because I need to.

Trashing these daily words lets me say my peace and get on with life.

You see... The blank page is the kindest permission and deepest forgiveness I have to offer myself and in turn, the world.

Handwritten? Typed?

There are strong advocates of doing stream-of-consciousness writing by hand, with paper and pen (or pencil.) But do you prefer spiral bound? Unlined? Graph paper? Separate sheets? Small pages? Massive pages? Pen or pencil? Or Marker?

In fact, don't limit yourself to one combination. Just remember that at the end of your writing session it's just a piece of paper with some words, possibly at the bottom of a trash can. You can pick a new combination tomorrow, if you want.

I've noticed a big difference between the kinds of thoughts and complete sentences that flow out of me on a piece of paper versus using the computer screen and a keyboard. Sometimes I'm not near a pen and a piece of paper and I have so many thoughts racing through my head, I need the speed of my typing to keep up with the river of chaos flowing out of my mind.

There are myriad writing apps you can pick from. As with pen and paper, do a little research to find the app you like best for writing. (There's a list of my favorite writing apps and tools in the book bonuses: http://emilyannpeterson.com/bnb-book)

Now that my essential tremor in my right hand is getting worse, I tend to lean more toward doing my daily expression with my laptop. Resting my hands and wrists prevents my arms from getting too exhausted from stabilization.

Express yourself in a native tongue.

Whether you stick with "analog" and write with pen and paper or venture into technology, just remember this: your selection of writing tools should foster free-flowing expression. So if you're bilingual, this might mean writing in "Spanglish" or "Frenglish."

Use a timer.

During really busy seasons of life, I use the timer as one of my writing tools. On days that I've woken wracked with fear about a concert coming up, I know writing about it will be the best gift I can give everyone in the audience. But as with most mornings before a performance there are so many things I have to do!

Unfortunately I don't have the luxury of time to write for hours. But I do have 15 minutes. So setting the timer allows my brain to relax into the freedom of expression just a little bit more by not being worried about time.

Remember, the goal is find the tools that foster your fluency and ease of practice.

Maybe your best tools include a cup of coffee and a warm pair of socks? If you have any favorite tools to add, be sure to share with the class! (Tag me on social media so I can give you a shout-out!)

The Basics of Building Bravery with Expression

Expression onto the impermanent page through stream-of-consciousness writing might be the most radical act of bravery in existence.

When you're alone in the mountains, with no real future for your career, not very many friends left to help, with things looking very very bleak - I can tell you from experience that expression can be the thing that pulls you through.

When you've hidden your pain so well that no one knows you're this close to dying from physical self-harm - again, from experience, I can tell you expression might be the only thing that pulls you through safely.

When your depression has you chained indoors (been there, done that) if nothing else, expression will give you something else to do other than stare at the ceiling. But most likely, expression will be the thing that snaps you out of a frozen cycle of fuzzy-headed vision.

Crawling through the rubble of your life through self-expression might not change the immediate present, but it can be your source of life as you move forward. And although expression may not seem like a very creative option when you're laid out amongst the rubble or when you can feel the walls caving in from the weight of your constraints, let me tell you it is.

I've felt my esophagus start to clamp shut and my lack of control slip through my fingers. By expressing myself in those moments, I am able to find the shreds of my real self, the same shreds required for Bare Naked Bravery.

When the walls are caving in, you have a bajillion unread emails from your boss, someone keeps texting you with updates about the crisis at hand, the person sitting next to you on the bus is listening to the most godawful music on the planet, and the person on the other side of you is talking on the phone to their nagging mother-in-law ... Screaming "SHUT UP!" sounds like a phenomenal idea, right? Or maybe getting off the bus entirely? Whatever you end up doing, that is expression in the midst of constraint.

What's the first thing that happens after you've dropped and shattered the cocktail glass? Probably a four-letter word, right? Boom. Expression in the midst of constraint.

When you're having the kind of panic attack that makes all other panic attacks want to have a panic attack, calling 911 is a form of expression. But so is that silly (but very effective) exercise of just sitting and feeling it all. Oh and breathing. Creating helps a lot. By taking the time to connect your physical feelings with your emotions in a mindful way, that is expression too.

The expression of your constraints unties the pressure that's been building up. Expression is the release valve.

Bravery Building Tool #2: Feel it.

I received many pieces of therapeutic advice during my eating disorder recovery. One suggestion just seemed so stupid. I honestly heard it the first time and rolled my eyes. My eyes rolled so hard, it was almost audible. I was certain it wasn't going to work. I was certain it was just my therapist grasping at straws, a last ditch effort to distract me from self-harm.

But it was spot-on.

The advice is this: "Just sit there. Close your eyes. Breathe. And observe the feelings. The emotions will come in waves. They will appear in various parts of your body. They'll move to other parts of your body. Just keep breathing and observing until they subside and you feel ready to open your eyes."

The only objective with this exercise was to tie my emotions to their physical sensations. I began to notice emotions had repeatable and identifiable physical sensations. Fear rested on my chest like a heavy non-purring panther. Loneliness felt like ten layers of heavy and immovable x-ray vests from the dentist office. Betrayal would sting my shoulders and grief would burn and pulse hot sorrow through my arms.

I don't know about you, but awful feelings would tend to get me when I was alone and tired. So most of the time, I did this exercise at night. I would sit there in bed, with quiet tears streaming down my face, observing the intensity and color of emotion coursing through my veins and feeling whatever wave of emotion would pass through my arms and then legs.

Normally, I'd unintentionally fall asleep and wake up with puffy eyes and a stuffy nose from crying. But it never failed. When the exercise (or my slumber) was complete, my constraints had been utilized by feeling my emotions fully and listening to them.

The beauty of this simple exercise is this: Using expressive mindfulness, somewhere within the discomfort, I can always find my bravery.

I've done this exercise outdoors with a raucous house party on the inside. Bravery will remind me that I can leave the party. I'm not trapped there. But sometimes doing this exercise will remind me that I actually enjoy my friends and I really do want to stay.

I've done this exercise in the car after a performance (or before a speaking engagement). After the wave of feeling overwhelmed passes, I find bravery waiting and able to remind me why I chose to say yes to the event in the first place.

I've done this exercise in the guest bedroom waiting for my familial fury to subside. Often what remains is remembering how freakin' adorable my nieces are and how much I really do love my family, despite all of our differences and mutual failures.

Sometimes feelings will get too powerful and this exercise will prompt ways to ask for company and help from someone I trust. And sometimes the bravery is simply found in this exercise through the rediscovery of the fact that the fear will subside (even if it's just a little bit) by morning.

I still practice this exercise in multiple forms. Sometimes it looks like walking the dog. Sometimes it looks like writing. Sometimes it looks like songwriting. Sometimes it looks like playing a simple musical scale.

Not-so-surprisingly I've taught a similar exercise to every student and client. We go through it at the start of every lesson and meeting. For my business clients, we do a check-in, a basic "how are things going?" Sometimes we do a longer grounding exercise or a small meditation. Sometimes we make a list of things on our mind to discuss throughout the meeting.

For my music/songwriting/creative students, We play or sing a scale. It's basic. It's a warm up. It's an exercise.

It's like reciting the ABC's. Most music teachers require the practice of scales from their students. But not every teacher introduces this practice as an exercise in expressive mindfulness. You guessed it, I'm not every teacher. So we start the lesson as follows...

[First note] How are my feet today? Flat? Relaxed? Tense?
[Second note] How are my legs today? Strong? Noodles? Tight?
[Third note] How are my hips? Steady? Relaxed?
[Fourth note] How is my torso? Confident? Soft?
[Fifth note] How are my shoulders? Perched and upright? Even?
[Sixth note] What do my arms feel like today? Open? Mighty?
[Seventh note] What's my brain like? Is it crazy? Placid?
[Eighth note] How is my breathing? Fast? Slow? Shallow? Deep?
[Ninth note, reversing the scale] Repeat questions.

Regardless of the intention of the session (music, creativity, writing, business) the goal of this exercise is not to "fix" something in our physical or emotional posture. The goal is to merely notice what our bodies naturally want to do that particular day. We're acknowledging the constraints we're working within for that lesson (or practice session). We're checking to see how much the stress of the workday or school day is leaning into our time together. We're exploring the sensations and ramifications of our constraints and allowing ourselves to resonate within them.

Bravery Building Tool #3: Meditation

Meditation gives us the space not only to watch our thoughts and emotions pass by, but it heightens our ability to be sensitive without judgment. This can become one of our greatest strengths in pursuit of a brave life.

This makes it a perfect practice tool for bravery. We need heightened sensitivity to enhance our improvisational impulses. We need silence to acknowledge the contrasting noise within our context and environment. We need to know how to access the stability of our physical and emotional body and that we can access that stability with every breath.

If you're new to meditation or you find yourself rolling your eyes or tempted to skip to the next bravery building tool, I encourage you to explore meditation like we can explore our bravery through writing or any other tool: with judgment-free, frequency, fluency, and curious impermanence.

Try giving yourself the impermanence of five to 10 minutes. To minimize distraction and increase your fluency of this practice, go find a quiet place. Set a timer so your mind doesn't have to hold on to keeping track of time. Close your eyes. Wear a blindfold to block visual lighting distractions. Count your breaths backward from 10. If you lose track of which number you're on, go back to 10. If you reach the number 1, go back to 10. While you're doing this, notice if any random thoughts bubble up. When they do, see what happens if you metaphorically "let go" of each thought like a balloon tied to the next breath.

There are so many tools out there for meditation. Guided meditations can help ground and center a hectic mind to find the honesty of your bravery. Guided visualizations can inspire and provoke your vision of possibility and imagination within your bravery. And as with the previously mentioned writing practice tool, there are helpful technologies and apps available to build and teach meditation.

If you'd like to get started, there is a free meditation audio in your Book Bonuses. (Download here: http://emilyannpeterson.com/bnb-book)

Bravery Building Tool #4: Masterminds & Shared Experiences

Ask any artists who crowdfunded their creative projects, you'll hear how terrifying that process is. Laying your heart and art on the line for all to see, asking them, "Do you value this as much as I do?" Crowdfunding is a brutal bootcamp for bravery. And yet...

I am such a huge advocate for crowdsourcing your practice of bravery. The book you're reading right now is a result of the combined support and encouragement I've received from my own bravery crowdsourcing.

Masterminds

Not as brutal as crowdfunding is the practice of gathering with a small group of fellow creatives and bravery builders. The business world call these groups "masterminds." Essentially, they are small groups of people gathering with the same intention.

Personally, I've done these small groups with

- 2 other musician friends who want to build a monthly patronage program
- 3 other podcasters who want to learn from and keep each other accountable in producing kick-ass interviews
- 8 other women business owners who want to transform their hustle into creative flow
- 4 other songwriters who want to get really good at their storytelling craft.

Sometimes these groups are lead by a coach or mentor. Sometimes they're peer-led. Leading and facilitating Bravery Masterminds is one of the great honors of my career. If you're curious, check out http://emilyannpeterson.com/masterminds for more info.

For you this might mean going through this book with a couple of friends. (Check the book club guide in your book bonuses! http://emilyannpeterson.com/bnb-book) Or join one of the groups I facilitate for my clients. We'd love to have you, if there's room and if you're the right fit.

If you're interested in what a group looks like, here are time-tested methods for building a sustainable and helpful mastermind group:

- Gather two to eight other folks who are willing to help each other build bravery (perhaps in a certain area of life?) who also have similar intentions and similar expectations.

- Agree to meet at a certain frequency. I find that weekly is best.

- Agree to have an official "end date" so things don't get awkward when someone has to bow out eventually and so everyone knows they have the same commitment level to the group.

- Create a structure for how you want to divide the time. Take turns every week? Rotate monthly? My favorite is 15-20 minutes per person each week, but that's not always feasible for larger groups.

- If it's your turn to be in the "hot seat" be honest about your struggles and open to hearing advice and encouragement from your fellow group members.

- Also important, be willing to ask and answer the hard questions.

- Designate a "Keeper of the Time." This is especially helpful if everyone gets a turn each week. Respecting everyone's time is just part of being a good group member.

- The best results I've seen from these groups happen when each person has a "homework assignment" or something to complete before the next meeting. Most of the time these assignments arise naturally in conversation.

- Be prepared to take notes or record the meeting to go back and reference later. (This is one of the reasons I love video conferencing so much.)

- If you find yourself in an ongoing group with no end date, I recommend setting quarterly or yearly themes so attention doesn't go stagnant.

Magical things happen because of groups like this. Keeping each other accountable and leaning on each other for support is crucial, especially if you want to build authentic vulnerability, big imagination, and keen improvisational skills. Sometimes growing bravery requires a small and trusted army of encouragement.

Sharing experiences with others can be the most powerful way to build bravery. This doesn't have to happen in a mastermind group.

Sometimes it's as simple as smashing pumpkins. Allow me to explain...

Shared Experiences

The period from 2013-2014 was particularly bad for me. Don't get me wrong there were amazing and beautiful things that came out of that season of externally prompted bravery, but holy cow. I had a breakup with a boyfriend. My best friend got married and moved to Dallas. My car kept getting hit while parked outside my house. I had several workplace scenarios that left me feeling sorely undervalued. I was fighting loneliness. Bandmates vanished on me and left me out of a creative project. I was no longer doing work I had a passion for and instead working a day job that sucked the ever-loving soul from my bones. I was beginning to drown in debt and one of my favorite former cello students had just told me they were battling cancer. Oh, and a health diagnosis of my own was wreaking havoc on my life.

October held the straw that broke the back of this whole season: Someone broke into the church where I was renting studio space, kicked down my office door, and stole my laptop.

I broke. I mean I really broke down. After wiping the tears from my face, I got this crazy idea to buy one pumpkin for each of the lousy things that happened over the previous year and smash it.

Knowing two days later my good friends Kye and Melanie were hosting their annual October chili cook-off, I asked Melanie if it was alright to have a "Smashing of the Pumpkins" event in addition to their chili contest. We opened the invitation to anyone at the party who might want to join in smashing their problems to bits. I promised there would be tarps, baseball bats, and Sharpies. It was a BYOP situation.

It was a plan. Pumpkins were gonna get *smashed*.

I arrived to the chili cook-off early with the 12 doomed pumpkins of my own. We lined them up and I carefully wrote one thing on each with a scrawl of permanent marker.

It was never my intention for this to be a solo performance art event. I was so angry that I was fully expecting other folks to bring their own pumpkins to deposit their feelings. But it looked like I was the only person with pumpkins at this party. Twelve of them to be exact.

So gripping the baseball bat with a thread of hesitation and a nervous smile, I exclaimed to the whole barbeque, "Can I have your attention please? So ... this was a really shitty year. A lot of awful things happened and I thought it'd be a good idea to take my anger to a pumpkin. Please join in if you are so led."

With everyone looking around now also uncomfortable and standing/sitting at an equally uncomfortable distance away from me, I continued, "This," holding up the first doomed pumpkin with the word UNDERVALUED, "is for everyone who feels overlooked."

Placing the little pumpkin in the center of the tarp, I took a step back and a deep breath. SMACK. The baseball bat slapped that little pumpkin like a wimpy insult. It turns out that small, fresh-off-the-vine pumpkins aren't so easy to smash, so I put some more leg muscle into it.

About 6 baseball bat whacks in, a FLOODGATE of anger opened and I became a rage machine. One pumpkin down, 11 to go.

A friend placed the next pumpkin on the tarp. "This one is for boyfriends rightfully leaving you for their dream job halfway around the world," I shouted while summoning power from my toes to bring down onto this poor pumpkin with the word "Iceland" on it.

Smashing pumpkins is a lot harder than it sounds. These were no rotting jack o'lanterns, these were fresh, whole pumpkins from the farm down the road. And yet, pumpkin innards were flying. The baseball bat was slimy. My face was red and I could feel adrenaline pulsing through my body.

The entire chili cook-off just turned into something none of us had expected and something none of us knew what to label. But it was too late to turn back now. After finishing off "Iceland," I turned around and grabbed the next pumpkin, "Laptop Stolen."

One after another, I smashed them. To smithereens. The chili crowd was now cheering at the pumpkins representing their own misery.

Car repairs.
Day job.
Loneliness.
Debt.

My back had now joined the yelling alongside the rest of the chili cook-off, only it wasn't cheering. It was screaming at me to stop before I seriously strained something. So by the time I finished stomping on the "Cancer" pumpkin, I was beginning to slow down and lose steam.

The crowd of friends circled around me were now cinched closer to the tarp of pumpkin doom, despite the amount of slimy pumpkin getting flung everywhere. There was a buzz in the air that felt like a pressing question, "Where is this gonna go next?!"

One pumpkin remained.

The biggest, monstrous pumpkin was waiting with the words "Essential Tremor" written across the front. I took a couple of deep breaths while I heard strangers and acquaintances muttering "Huh? What's that mean?" As I took the first swing at this last pumpkin, I heard a friend telling them, "She has this tremor in her hand and now she can't play the cello like she used to."

With those words, suddenly I was too tired. After 11 pumpkins, you'd have felt the same way. I couldn't take another swing at the rest of this 75 percent smashed pumpkin. A friend grabbed the bat from my hands and stepped onto the tarp while laughing about how slimy it was. I caught my breath and strained a smile with my hands on my hips as he wiped the handle clean with the bottom corner of his t-shirt.

He had the same experience with this first whack. Not very satisfying. He laughed again and gripped the baseball bat like an axe and then squatted down like he was a lumberjack getting ready to do some full-body wood splitting.

He *laid* into this pumpkin. And how. It took precisely five attempts to finish off the remainder of that last pumpkin.

The sight of this friend was jarring. There he was wailing on the pumpkin that represented the biggest, most life-altering, awful thing that happened to me all year. Even though I had already demolished 11 pumpkins, he was so strong. I felt so weak in comparison.

Seeing that was all I needed. In an instant my rageful steam turned into a puddle of grief.

There, in front of friends, acquaintances, and strangers, I was covered head-to-toe in pumpkin slime and my chin began to quiver. Another friend saw me melting into tears and pressed my face into her shoulder. She denied my apology for getting her covered in pumpkin slime and snot. While patting my back she said, "We've got you."

That night became a metaphor for how important community and connection is for our seasons of bravery. We can wail all we want and pour sheer amounts of willpower into "fixing" things just so.

Mustering the fake strength to "press on" and "do it anyway." We can erect rituals, rules, and boundaries. We can hustle till we are red and tight-in-the-face.

But sharing experiences, built on vulnerability, imagination, and improvisation, is what really builds bravery. In my personal experience, sharing these moments with others makes for the most powerful expressions of Bare Naked Bravery.

I know this because the lawn which held this Inaugural Pumpkin Smashing produced tiny pumpkin plants for at least three Octobers symbolizing new life and fresh starts.

You certainly don't have to go around asking people to join in on an Annual Smashing of the Pumpkins. Although, it *was* cathartic and delightfully strange for everyone involved. However, I do recommend sending out some vulnerable invitations to someone else who might have more strength to offer your circumstance.

It is my hope and prayer that we can all build our bravery, *together*. For that is what makes bravery contagious, and worth it. Most of all, we need your bravery. We need you to stand up about something, speak up when it's not the easiest, and show up ready for movement. That's how anger and fear turns into sorrow, and sorrow melts into bravery, and bravery into love.

Appendix A: Bravery Boosting Questions

The next time you're facing a "brave moment" and need an extra boost of creative courage, I highly recommend answering these questions. Write them out or talk them through internally. Take lots of deep breaths while finding the answers.

A "prettier" version of these are available to download in your book bonuses here: http://emilyannpeterson. com/bnb-book

1. On a scale of 1-10 how honest am I being right now?
2. What's really at stake here?
3. What do I wish I could say?
4. Where is the precise edge of my comfort-zone?
5. Where are the actual limitations in this situation?
6. If the stars aligned perfectly, what can I expect?
7. When/what was the last time/thing I created?

8. What is realistically possible?

9. Where do I feel the most friction in this situation?

10. What is my gut telling me?

11. Where is my power of choice?

12. When is my gut telling me to use that power of choice?

Appendix B: Book Club Guide

Grab some trusted friends (or total strangers?) and start a book club! Here's how I suggest running these, but obviously do whatever feels like the appropriate thing to do, especially if strangers are involved. ;-)

1. Download your copy of the Book Club Guide in the Book Bonuses available here: http://emilyannpeterson.com/bnb-book

2. Each section of the Book Club Guide has "homework" and group questions to discuss.

3. Bonus: If you do get a group together, I want to know about it! A simple email will do, but a big group selfie would make my day! Feel free to send along any extra questions if you like.

Appendix C: Recommended Resources

Further reading, lectures, videos, articles, and apps are available in your book bonuses!

Get your book bonuses by visiting:
http://emilyannpeterson.com/bnb-book

Appendix D: Lyrics

All lyrics written by Emily Ann Peterson (BMI)

Now that most of my music-listening happens digitally, I don't often get the opportunity to consume my songwriting colleagues new lyrics like I wish I could. If you're like me, then you enjoy reading the the lyrics too. Just in case you fall into that category, here lyrics of songs I've written inspired by moments of bravery.

Horton's Hope

last night, you fell out of the sky
I saw you gently land upon a clover
you were safe, you were heard, you were here.
your voice, the only thing I knew of you

there I held you in my hand
just a speck of whisper from your voice
you were safe, you were heard, you were here
we found worlds beyond our own

covered in clover, I'm listening
going through them one by one
covered in clover I'm listening
please don't make yourself at home
covered in clover, I can't hear you anymore

they said, my mind was out of joint
but you were safely sitting on a clover
pointed fingers, leaning shoulders
and the dark side of their shoes
I watched them fly you from my hold

covered in clover, I'm listening
going through them one by one
covered in clover I'm listening
please don't make yourself at home
covered in clover, I can't hear you anymore

maybe we, we'll be saved
by the smallest of them all
maybe we, we'll be saved
by the smallest of them all

covered in clover, I'm listening
going through them one by one
covered in clover I'm listening
please don't make yourself at home
covered in clover, I can't hear you anymore

We Need Tonight

I had quite the month,
making Christmas music in October
I didn't get out much
so I'm feeling a little crazy in my head

my OCD came out to play

I'm looking forward to tonight
although my social anxiety might, not be
but screw it I'm here and you're here too.
I'm glad to not feel so alone

oh my god, what a week
what with traffic and customers whining
you had deadlines to meet
but the client from hell didn't help.

I'm so glad you're here

you need tonight
I can see that you're wound kinda tight
the kids are at home, Netflix can wait
your boss won't call 'cause your phone's turned off
tonight you won't feel so alone

it's not that easy, being alive
might not get better, better with time

oh how we need tonight
'cause the war's got no end in sight
the yelling gets louder 'cause no one will listen
so the walls just get higher but hate just spreads
when bombs have dropped and crying won't stop

we need to not feel so alone
we need to not feel so alone
I need to not feel so alone
you need to not feel so alone
we need to not feel so alone

A Little Bit

one day ago
two eyes welled up
three tears of joy rolled down
I would see you soon.

four hours passed
and then five minutes more
then with six beats of my heart all at once
I knew I loved you.

you're just a little bit right now
with little bitty hands and toes
you're a little bit new right now
all of me knows, all of me loves you

you are seven states away
eight trains from here.
nine unicorns couldn't fly fast enough
when you're not here

'cause your ten fingers and toes
couldn't count eleven arms of love
and twelve elephant ears couldn't hear
how much I love you

I'm a little bit far right now
a little more than far from hello
I'm a little bit far right now
but all of me knows, all of me loves you

when thirteen months go by
or fourteen hairs of mine are gray
if you are fifteen inches taller than me
I will still love you

the next sixteen sweet short years
might hold seventeen roses with thorns
but there are eighteen people are pulling for you
you're not alone

you're a little bit young right now
even though you're small, you'll grow
you're a little bit young right now
all of us knows, all of us loves you

you're a little bit of your daddy
a little bit of your momma
a little bit of your aunties
a little bit of your sister
and everyone else agrees

all of us know, all of us loves you
all of us know, all of us loves you

Tell Me Again

where are the girls mounted above me,
who failed to give up every stone?
who prove there's a way love can resolve
all the backdoors, hushed notes, and bones?
I hear you list every way I don't seem to fit
outline my should be, thin now thick then

you tell me again
tell me again
how I cannot belong
you tell me again

perfectly marred, who would unwrap me
wounded walls and all my sacred masking?
can I be loved? would you even want me to?
is there hope for my heart? maybe I convince you
to lean on my strength, head strong on my thigh
press into my flaws, drink me in and sigh, then

you tell me again
tell me again
there's no hope for my heart
you tell me again

so are there boxes my size, curved & wide?
would the corners give way for my love?
I ask while you sleep in my neck, breath in my ear
full weight on my chest, wake from your hollow
deep

tell me again
tell me again
all this time you were wrong
tell me again.

Velveteen

love stirred, in my sawdust heart
button eyes and a soft pink nose
velvet skin, with hidden seams
life-sized dreams underneath

love stirred, from fairy huts
of berry canes on those summer days
he was young, I was so naive.
you wouldn't think we could be

hopeful & fragile
hopeful & fragile
will his love make me real?

love grew and settled down
shape & shine, forgotten now
velveteen worn down smooth
there's a spot from days that soothe

love said, I'm beautiful
even though it's not what others see
everyday is how you're made
becoming real pink will fade

threadbare & fragile
threadbare & fragile
will his love let me last?
will it last?

hello, come sit with me
for now, I don't want to dance
please know, he meant everything he said
you will find....

I'm real & fragile
I'm real & fragile
will his love give me legs to walk away?

Shade of Silver

edges ache
ribs break inside out
from black and white fences

should you ever need
someone standing by your side
I'll be right here tugging on the line

we're all a shade of silver
inbetweens hold everything
yes is overrated.
no is overrated.
so maybe...

quilting pins
take the magic from the sky
fear will freeze your heart

we're all a shade of silver
inbetweens hold everything
yes is overrated.
no is overrated.
so maybe...

when your gray
starts to seem too blue
I'll be right here standing next to you

we're all a shade of silver
inbetweens hold everything
yes is overrated.
no is overrated.
so maybe...

Bruise Easy

when we said our goodbyes, I heard the silence start to ring
when we said our goodbyes, I felt my cheek begin to sting
I was bracing for the blow, but it hit me hard
adrenaline was pumping and it hit me hard

don't worry, I still sing
my chest is tight but I can still breathe
go on, I'll be just fine
I may bruise easy, but we didn't break a thing

you left just in time for my heart to still beat on its own
you left just in time for the ache to stay dull in my bones
I was bracing for the blow, but it hit me hard
adrenaline was pumping and it hit me hard
don't worry, I still sing
my chest is tight but I can still breathe
go on, I'll be just fine
I may bruise easy, but we didn't break a thing

the room stopped spinning, I'm still standing
I'm almost steady now, steady now
the room stopped spinning, I'm still standing
I'm almost steady now, steady now

don't worry, I still sing
my chest is tight but I can still breathe
go on, I'll be just fine
I may bruise easy, but we didn't break a thing

Other Woman

I don't want to be the other woman
but you call me when your sheets are cold
it's not me you really want now
she just won't hold you anymore

she can't bear to feel you close
she froze all the warmth of your days
here you are knocking at my door.
take this blanket, don't be cold anymore.

I stand strong. I will hold my ground.
I might be just another woman

I don't want to be the other woman
arrows draw—one black, one blue
I can see, names are rarely choice now
'cause I've got scarlett on my chest

she can't bear to feel you close
she froze all the warmth of your days
here you are knocking at my door.
take this blanket, don't be cold anymore.

I stand strong. I will hold my ground.
I might be just another woman
I stand strong. I will hold my ground.
I might be just another woman...

but I won't be your other woman.

Safe

don't step near me
don't you touch me so kind
I thought I told you, walk away.
don't you trust? I said I love you today.
no I won't hold you, just back away.

you're just not safe, near me.
there's a long list of reasons why
I'm just not safe, near you.
I can't love you like you want me to
I can't love you like I wanted to.

I'm on my own now.
It's not ideal, but I'll live.
we took our chances, we're better off alone.
I hope you find it
all the love there is to give
mine's not enough for you to call your own.

it'd be easier to stay if you were safe
it'd be easier to stay if I were safe with you

you're just not safe, near me.
there's a long list of reasons why
I'm just not safe, near you.
I can't love you like you want me to
I can't love you like I wanted to.

Tide's Turning

broken bottles down the hall,
fits of rage and alcohol
streaks of mean, all he was
when I was just a girl

mama had enough one day,
she packed our bags and we drove away
signed the papers late one night,
daddy was no more

tide's turning darling
I'm here to stay
hold my hand
you can breathe the fear away

on my uncle's family farm
I helped my cousins out in the barn
while mama worked her job downtown,
our blue grass turned pink

'cause mama one day met a tall marine
who went to war at seventeen
he returned to Michigan
his job brought him to town

he picked my mama up one night
I cracked the door, he seemed alright
a rose for mom and a doll for me
with a twinkle in her eye mama said

tide's turning darling
he's here to stay
hold my hand

you can breathe the fear away

after graduation gowns I got a good job
and I found
a man who loved me oceans deep
we said "I do" in Spring

wasn't long 'til we were three
a baby girl in my belly
I was terrified to let love in
but I was soon set straight, mama said

tide's turning darling
she's here to stay
hold her hand
you can breathe the fear away.

Seasons changed and years they went.
My mama always stayed my friend
Through sunday suppers and holidays
with the family gathered round

But mama one day told her tall marine
time was up, she was seeing things
They couldn't do much more
so I saw her every day

Mama's new home had a place to cry
when I couldn't stand to see her lying
in a bed that wouldn't hold her strength
even if she tried. Mama said

tide's turning darling
she's here to stay
hold her hand

you can breathe the fear away

Simple Words

simple words, we speak them young as told
seek and break em, til we're old
simple words, the kind that give and heal
cast like summer steel
simple words, everything can change
stones can melt and burst to flame, with these
simple words

I do. I love. I choose.
I choose you my love.

empty hands, all I have to give
nothing but my life to live
pockets filled, or inside out and down
either way simple words will sound, out into the
night

time may come and go…
even still I know…
these words will stand

I do. I love. I choose.
I choose you my love.

Gratitude

Thank you to my family. I do love you. So much.

Thank you to Renae Graves, Eden Smith-Hyder, April Arevalo, Melanie Harding, Kye Alfred Hillig, Jennifer & Scott Haydon, Jennifer Monahan, Chris Mathews Jr., Sara Erickson, Nick Herring, John Teske, Trapper Lukaart, Heidi Stoermer, Jan Krist, Alexandra Harbushka, and Mandy Troxel. I needed your bravery. Thank you for accepting the challenge.

Thank you to my bad ass team. Thank you to my editors Lisa Christman and Donna Capodeluco. Thank you to my publicist Victoria Shockley and assistants Chido Samantha and Alana Brown. Thank you to my podcast production team: Mike Lalonde, Karen Lindsay, and Darrell Darnell. You help spread bravery far & wide. You push me to be braver than I thought I could be. You magically turn my messy middles into truly joyful experiences.

Thank you to my patrons, clients, and fans: your courageous celebration of bravery blows my mind. I am so proud to know each of you and witness your bravery unfold daily. It is an honor of a lifetime.

About the Author

Emily Ann Peterson is a singer/songwriter, author, and creative consultant based out of the Pacific Northwest.

Emily writes for people who struggle to remember what hope feels like and sings to those who yearn for something secret. She speaks to those who are done being bored and crave all things beautiful, strong, sacred, and sensual. Her mission is to inspire a global resonance through the marriage of art and whole-person development.

Learn more about Emily and hear her music at www.emilyannpeterson.com.

CPSIA information can be obtained
at www.ICGtesting.com
Printed in the USA
FFOW03n0859210218
45096278-45531FF